How to do Accounting II

INSTRUCTORS SOLUTIONS
Table of Contents

by James Foote

©2005 TX 6-255-315

How to do Accounting II
INSTRUCTORS SOLUTIONS

10.1

Maeve's Magic Make-over
GENERAL JOURNAL

	DESCRIPTION	PR	DEBIT	CREDIT
1	Wages & Salary Expense		1,973.54	
2	FIT Payable			246.92
3	FICA Payable			122.36
4	Medicare Payable			28.62
5	401-K - Rowe & Rowe Payable			20.00
6	United Way Payable			20.00
7	Cash - Payroll			1,535.64
8				
9	Cash - Payroll		1,535.64	
10	Cash			1,535.64
11				
12				

10.3

Gail's Goods
GENERAL JOURNAL

	DESCRIPTION	PR	DEBIT	CREDIT
1	Wages & Salary Expense		1,672.75	
2	FIT Payable			191.79
3	FICA Payable			103.71
4	Medicare Payable			24.25
5	State & Local Taxes Payable			62.44
6	United Way Payable			17.00
7	Cash - Payroll			1,273.56
8				
9	Cash - Payroll		1,273.56	
10	Cash			1,273.56
11				
12				
13				
14				

Payroll Register
10.1 Maeve's 10.2 Gail's Goods

Maeve's Magic Make-over

NAME	EARNINGS			DEDUCTIONS					
10.1	Regular	Overtime	Total Pay	Fed Income Tx	Soc. Sec. Tax	Medicare Tax	401-K	United Way	Net Pay
Jacob Job	250.00	0.00	250.00	25.00	15.50	3.63	5	5	195.88
Mel Malone	350.00	39.38	389.38	46.73	24.14	5.65			312.86
Sandra S.	264.10	0.00	264.10	26.41	16.37	3.83			217.49
Sally Smith	370.00	20.81	390.81	46.90	24.23	5.67	15	5	294.02
Jennifer B.	572.00	107.25	679.25	101.89	42.11	9.85		10	515.40
Totals 10.1	$1,806.10	$167.44	$1,973.54	$246.92	$122.36	$28.62	$20.00	$20.00	$1,535.64

10.3

		Pay Rate	Tax Rate				
Jacob Job	40	6.25	0.10	0.062	0.0145	5	
Mel Malone	40	8.75	0.12				
Sandra S.	38	6.95	0.10				
Sally Smith	40	9.25	0.12			5	
Jennifer B.	40	14.3	0.15			10	

Gail's Goods

PAYROLL REGISTER

NAME	EARNINGS			DEDUCTIONS					
10.3	Regular	Overtime	Total Pay	Fed Income Tx	Soc. Sec. Tax	Medicare Tax	State	United Way	Net Pay
Jim Metro	336.00	0.00	336.00	40.32	20.83	4.87	13.44	10.00	246.54
Helen Lake	186.00	0.00	186.00	18.60	11.53	2.70	5.58		147.59
Joe Salt	220.00	41.25	261.25	26.13	16.20	3.79	7.84	2.00	205.30
Peg Pepper	370.00	55.50	425.50	51.06	26.38	6.17	17.02		324.87
Chris Jack	464.00	0.00	464.00	55.68	28.77	6.73	18.56	5.00	349.26
TOTALS 10.3	$1,576.00	$96.75	$1,672.75	$191.79	$103.71	$24.25	$62.44	$17.00	$1,273.56

10.3

		Pay Rate	Fed Income Tx	Other Taxes		
Jim Metro	40	8.4	0.12	FICA	0.062	
Helen Lake	24	7.75	0.10	Medical	0.0145	0.04	0.03
Joe Salt	40	5.5	0.10	State	0.03	0.03
Peg Pepper	40	9.25	0.12	City	0.01	0.04
Chris Jack	40	11.6	0.12	City & State	0.04	0.04

10.2

Mike Brandon
PAYROLL REGISTER
Date

NAME	EARNINGS			DEDUCTIONS					Net Pay
10.2	Regular	Overtime	Total Pay	Fed Income Tx	Soc. Sec. Tax	Medicare Tax	Child	United Way	
Shirley James	250.00	0	250.00	25.00	15.50	3.63	25	5	175.88
Liam Foote	260.00	29.25	289.25	28.93	17.93	4.19			238.20
Dick Reed	396.00	74.25	470.25	56.43	29.16	6.82		10	367.85
Karen Mallett	219.80	0	219.80	21.98	13.63	3.19	35		146.01
Tom Jones	99.00	0	99.00	9.90	6.14	1.44			81.53
Totals	$1,224.80	$103.50	$1,328.30	$142.24	$82.35	$19.26	$60.00	$15.00	$1,009.45

10.2

			Pay Rate	Fed Income Tax	Other Taxes	
Shirley James	40		6.25	0.10	FICA	0.062
Liam Foote	40	3	6.50	0.10	Medicare	0.0145
Dick Reed	40	5	9.90	0.12		
Karen Mallett	28		7.85	0.10		
Tom Jones	18		5.50	0.10		

Mike Brandon

| 10.2 | | | | | **CASH JOURNAL** | | | Page__1 |

	CASH		DATE		DESCRIPTION	Post	GENERAL	
	Debit	Credit	Month	Day		Ref	Debit	Credit
1	25,000.00		May	2	Mike Brandon, Capital	310		25,000.00
2		300.00		5	Rent Expense	535	300.00	
3		200.00		6	Office Supplies	120	200.00	
4				9	Purchases (Beginning Inventory)	125	100,000.00	
5					Note Payable (Lucky Guy)	250		100,000.00
6	85,000.00			13	Sales	410		85,000.00
7		2,500.00		15	Advertising Expense	520	2,500.00	
8					Wages/Salary Expense	550	1,328.30	
9					Federal Income Tax Payable	220		142.24
10					FICA Payable	222		82.35
11					Medicare Payable	225		19.26
12					Child Care Payable	230		60.00
13					United Way Payable	232		15.00
14					Cash - Payroll	115		1,009.45
15		1,009.45			Cash - Payroll	115	1,009.45	
16	4,900.00			20	Sales	410		4,900.00
17				21	Purchases	510	20,000.00	
18					Accounts Payable / Lee's	210		20,000.00
19		10,000.00			Note Payable (Lucky Guy)	250	10,000.00	
20		150.00		23	Utility Expense	540	150.00	
21		300.00		26	Mike Brandon, Drawing	320	300.00	
22	5,875.00			28	Sales	410		5,875.00
23		243.85		29	Federal Income Tax Payable	220	142.24	
24					FICA Payable	222	82.35	
25					Medicare Payable	225	19.26	
26		3,000.00		30	Accounts Payable / Lee's	210	3,000.00	
27								
28	120,775.00	17,703.30					139,031.60	242,103.30
30								
31	Prove Cash Journal							
32	Debit	Credit						
33	259,806.60	259,806.60						
34								
35								

Brandon's　　　General Ledger　　　Chapter 10 & 11

Account　　　　　　　　　　CASH　　　　　　　　　　No. 110

DATE		ITEM	PR	Debit	Credit	BALANCE Debit	BALANCE Credit
May	31		1	120,775.00			
	31				17,703.30	103,071.70	
June	30		3	17,057.00		0.00	
					21,710.08	98,418.62	

Account　　　　　　　　　　CASH - PAYROLL　　　　　　　　　　No.115

DATE		ITEM	PR	Debit	Credit	BALANCE Debit	BALANCE Credit
May	15		1	1,009.45		1,009.45	
	15		1		1,009.45	0.0	
June	1		2	971.55		971.6	
	1				971.55	0.0	
	15		2	1,000.80		1,000.80	
	15		2		1,000.80	0.00	
	30		3	1,187.73		1,187.73	
	30		3		1,187.73	0.00	

Account　　　　　　　　　　OFFICE SUPPLIES　　　　　　　　　　No.120

DATE		ITEM	PR	Debit	Credit	BALANCE Debit	BALANCE Credit
May	6		1	200.00		200.00	

Account　　　　　　　　　　INVENTORY　　　　　　　　　　No. 125

DATE		ITEM	PR	Debit	Credit	BALANCE Debit	BALANCE Credit
May	9	Beginning Inventory	1	100,000		100,000	

Account   ACCOUNTS PAYABLE   No. 210

DATE		ITEM	PR	Debit	Credit	BALANCE Debit	BALANCE Credit
May	21	Lee's	1		20,000.00		20,000.00
	29		1	3,000.00			17,000.00
June	11	Lee's	2		5,000		22,000.00
	17		3	5,000			17,000.00
	27		3	2,000			15,000.00

Account   FEDERAL INCOME TAX PAYABLE   No. 220

DATE		ITEM	PR	Debit	Credit	BALANCE Debit	BALANCE Credit
May	15		1		142.24		142.24
	29		1	142.24		0	
June	1		2		136.64		136.64
	15		2		141.19		277.83
	30		3		164.89		442.72

Account   FICA PAYABLE   No. 222

DATE		ITEM	PR	Debit	Credit	BALANCE Debit	BALANCE Credit
May	15		1		82.35		82.35
	29		1	82.35			0.00
June	1		2		82.35		82.35
	1		2		79.43		161.78
	1		2		79.43		241.21
	15		2		81.70		322.91
	15		2		81.70		404.61
	30		3		95.84		500.45
	30		3		95.84		596.29

Account   MEDICARE PAYABLE   No. 225

DATE		ITEM	PR	Debit	Credit	BALANCE Debit	BALANCE Credit
May	15		1		19.26		19.26
	29		1	19.26			0.00
June	1		2		19.26		19.26
	1		2		18.58		37.84
	1		2		18.58		56.42
	15		2		19.11		75.53
	15		2		19.11		94.64
	30		3		22.42		117.06
	30		3		22.42		139.48

Account | | | | CHILD CARE PAYABLE | | | No. 230

					BALANCE	
DATE		ITEM	PR	Debit	Credit	Debit	Credit
May	15		1		60.00		60.00
June	1		2		60.00		120.00
	15		2		60.00		180.00
	30		3		60.00		240.00

Account | | | | UNITED WAY PAYABLE | | | No. 232

					BALANCE	
DATE		ITEM	PR	Debit	Credit	Debit	Credit
May	15		1		15.00		15.00
June	1		2		15.00		30.00
	15		2		15.00		45.00
	30		3		15.00		60.00

Account | | | | FEDERAL UNEMPLOYMENT PAYABLE | | | No.240

					BALANCE	
DATE		ITEM	PR	Debit	Credit	Debit	Credit
June	1		2		106.26		106.26
	1		2		102.50		208.76
	15		2		105.42		314.18
	30		3		123.67		437.85

Account | | | | STATE UNEMPLOYMENT | | | No. 242

					BALANCE	
DATE		ITEM	PR	Debit	Credit	Debit	Credit
June	1		2		66.42		66.42
	1		2		64.06		130.48
	15		2		65.89		196.37
	30		3		77.29		273.66

Account | | | | NOTES PAYABLE | | | No. 250

					BALANCE	
DATE		ITEM	PR	Debit	Credit	Debit	Credit
May	9	Lucky Guy Bank	1		100,000		100,000
May	21		1	10,000			90,000
June	18	Lucky Guy Bank	3	10,000			80,000

Account   **MIKE BRANDON, CAPITAL**   **No. 310**

					BALANCE	
DATE	ITEM	PR	Debit	Credit	Debit	Credit
May	2	Beginning Capital	1		25,000.00		25,000.00

Account   **MIKE BRANDON, DRAWING**   **No. 320**

DATE		ITEM	PR	Debit	Credit	Debit	Credit
						BALANCE	
May	26		1	300		300	
June	26		3	250		550	

Account   **SALES**   **No. 410**

DATE		ITEM	PR	Debit	Credit	Debit	Credit
						BALANCE	
May	13		1		85,000.00		85,000.00
	20		1		4,900.00		89,900.00
	28		1		5,875.00		95,775.00
June	10		2		3,895.00		99,670.00
	16		3		5,384.00		105,054.00
	25		3		7,778.00		112,832.00

Account   **PURCHASES**   **No. 510**

DATE		ITEM	PR	Debit	Credit	Debit	Credit
						BALANCE	
May	21		1	20,000.00		20,000.00	
June	11		2	5,000.00		25,000.00	

Account   **ADVERTISING EXPENSE**   **No. 520**

DATE		ITEM	PR	Debit	Credit	Debit	Credit
						BALANCE	
May	15		1	2,500.00		2,500.00	
June	5		2	500.00		3,000.00	
	19		3	500.00		3,500.00	

Account			EMPLOYER TAX EXPENSE				No. 530

						BALANCE	
DATE		ITEM	PR	Debit	Credit	Debit	Credit
June	1		2	274.29		274.29	
	1		2	264.57		538.86	
	15		2	272.12		810.98	
	30		3	319.22		1,130.20	

Account			RENT EXPENSE				No. 535

						BALANCE	
DATE		ITEM	PR	Debit	Credit	Debit	Credit
May	5		1	300		300	
June	3		2	300		600	

Account			UTILITY EXPENSE				No. 540

						BALANCE	
DATE		ITEM	PR	Debit	Credit	Debit	Credit
May	23		1	150		150	

Account			WAGES & SALARY EXPENSE				No. 550

						BALANCE	
DATE		ITEM	PR	Debit	Credit	Debit	Credit
May	15		1	1,328.30		1,328.30	
June	1		2	1,281.20		2,609.50	
	15		2	1,317.80		3,927.30	
	30		3	1,545.88		5,473.18	

Account							No.

						BALANCE	
DATE		ITEM	PR	Debit	Credit	Debit	Credit

Maeve's Magic Mart

11.1

Taxable Earnings Table

Name	Accumulated Earnings	Earnings Pay Period	Unemploy Tax Earn	Amount Taxed	FUTA 0.08	SUTA 0.05	FICA Match FICA	Med
Jacob Job	6,885.00	250.00	115.00	115.00	9.20	5.75	15.50	3.63
Mel Malone	8,992.00	389.38	0.00		0.00	0.00	24.14	5.65
Sandra S	6,400.90	264.10	599.10	264.10	21.13	13.21	16.37	3.83
Sally Smith	10,593.55	390.81	0.00		0.00	0.00	24.23	5.67
Jennifer B	15,232.91	679.25	0.00		0.00	0.00	42.11	9.85
Total				379.10	30.41	19.01	122.35	28.63

Gail's Goods

11.3

Taxable Earnings Table

Name	Accumulated Earnings	Earnings Pay Period	Unemploy Tax Earn	Amount Taxed	FUTA 0.08	SUTA 0.05	FICA Match FICA	Med
Jim Metro	7,894.33	336.00	0.00		0.00	0.00	20.83	4.87
Helen Lake	6,200.35	186.00	799.65	186.00	14.88	9.30	11.53	2.70
Joe Salt	6,825.50	261.25	174.50	174.50	13.96	8.73	16.20	3.79
Peg Pepper	10,586.35	425.50	0.00		0.00	0.00	26.38	6.17
Chris Jack	12,389.32	464.00	0.00		0.00	0.00	28.77	6.73
			974.15	360.50	28.84	18.03	103.71	24.26

11.1

Maeve's Magic Make-over
GENERAL JOURNAL

	DESCRIPTION	PR	DEBIT	CREDIT
1	Employer Tax Expense		200.40	
2	FICA Taxes Payable			122.35
3	Medicare Taxes Payable			28.63
4	Federal Unemployment Taxes Pay			30.41
5	State Unemployment Taxes Payable			19.01
6				
7				
8				
9				
10				

11.3

Gail's Goods
GENERAL JOURNAL

	DESCRIPTION	PR	DEBIT	CREDIT
1	Employer Tax Expense		174.84	
2	FICA Taxes Payable			103.71
3	Medicare Taxes Payable			24.26
4	Federal Unemployment Taxes Pay			28.84
5	State Unemployment Taxes Payable			18.03
6				
7				
8				
9				
10				

11.2 for 10.2

Taxable Earnings Table

Name	Accumulated Earnings	Earnings Pay Period	Unemploy Tax Earn	Amount Taxed	FUTA 0.08	SUTA 0.05	FICA Match FICA	Med
Shirly J	0.00	250.00	7,000.00	250.00	20.00	12.50	15.50	3.63
Liam Foote	0.00	289.25	7,000.00	289.25	23.14	14.46	17.93	4.19
Dick Reed	0.00	470.25	7,000.00	470.25	37.62	23.51	29.16	6.82
Karen M	0.00	219.80	7,000.00	219.80	17.58	10.99	13.63	3.19
Tom Jones	0.00	99.00	7,000.00	99.00	7.92	4.95	6.14	1.44
				1,328.30	106.26	66.42	82.36	$19.27

11.2

Taxable Earnings Table

Name	Accumulated Earnings	Earnings Pay Period	Unemploy Tax Earn	Amount Taxed	FUTA 0.08	SUTA 0.05	FICA Match FICA	Med
Shirly J	250.00	250.00	6,750.00	250.00	20.00	12.50	15.50	3.63
Liam Foote	289.25	260.00	6,710.75	260.00	20.80	13.00	16.12	3.77
Dick Reed	470.25	425.70	6,529.75	425.70	34.06	21.29	26.39	6.17
Karen M	219.80	235.50	6,780.20	235.50	18.84	11.78	14.60	3.41
Tom Jones	99.00	110.00	6,901.00	110.00	8.80	5.50	6.82	1.60
		1,281.20		1,281.20	102.50	64.06	79.43	18.58

11.2

Taxable Earnings Table

Name	Accumulated Earnings	Earnings Pay Period	Unemploy Tax Earn	Amount Taxed	FUTA 0.08	SUTA 0.05	FICA Match FICA	Med
Shirly J	500.00	268.75	6,500.00	268.75	21.50	13.44	16.66	3.90
Liam Foote	549.25	260.00	6,450.75	260.00	20.80	13.00	16.12	3.77
Dick Reed	895.95	470.25	6,104.05	470.25	37.62	23.51	29.16	6.82
Karen M	455.30	219.80	6,544.70	219.80	17.58	10.99	13.63	3.19
Tom Jones	209.00	99.00	6,791.00	99.00	7.92	4.95	6.14	1.44
				1,317.80	105.42	65.89	81.71	19.12

11.2

Taxable Earnings Table

Name	Accumulated Earnings	Earnings Pay Period	Unemploy Tax Earn	Amount Taxed	FUTA 0.08	SUTA 0.05	FICA Match FICA	Med
Shirly J	768.75	296.88	6,231.25	296.88	23.75	14.84	18.41	4.30
Liam Foote	809.25	279.50	6,190.75	279.50	22.36	13.98	17.33	4.05
Dick Reed	1,366.20	514.80	5,633.80	514.80	41.18	25.74	31.92	7.46
Karen M	675.10	251.20	6,324.90	251.20	20.10	12.56	15.57	3.64
Tom Jones	308.00	203.50	6,692.00	203.50	16.28	10.18	12.62	2.95
		1,545.88	31,072.70	1,545.88	123.67	77.29	95.85	22.40

Brandon's Payroll Register
May 15

NAME	EARNINGS			DEDUCTIONS						
10.2	Regular	Overtime	Total Pay	Fed Income Tx	Soc. Sec. Tax	Medicare Tax	Child	United Way	Net Pay
Shirley James	250.00	0	250.00	25.00	15.50	3.63	25	5	175.88
Liam Foote	260.00	29.25	289.25	28.93	17.93	4.19			238.20
Dick Reed	396.00	74.25	470.25	56.43	29.16	6.82		10	367.85
Karen Mallett	219.80	0	219.80	21.98	13.63	3.19	35		146.01
Tom Jones	99.00	0	99.00	9.90	6.14	1.44			81.53
Totals	$1,224.80	$103.50	$1,328.30	$142.24	$82.35	$19.26	$60.00	$15.00	$1,009.45

10.2		Pay Rate	Fed Income Tax	Other Taxes	
Shirley James	40		6.25	0.10	FICA	0.062
Liam Foote	40	3	6.50	0.10	Medicare	0.0145
Dick Reed	40	5	9.90	0.12		
Karen Mallett	28		7.85	0.10		
Tom Jones	18		5.50	0.10		

Employers Tax Expense

FUTA	0.08	$106.26
SUTA	0.05	$66.42

Brandon's Payroll Register
May 30

NAME	EARNINGS			DEDUCTIONS						
11.2	Regular	Overtime	Total Pay	Fed Income Tx	Soc. Sec. Tax	Medicare Tax	Child	United Way	Net Pay
Shirley James	250.00	0	250.00	25.00	15.50	3.63	25	5	175.88
Liam Foote	260.00	0	260.00	26.00	16.12	3.77			214.11
Dick Reed	396.00	29.70	425.70	51.08	26.39	6.17		10	332.05
Karen Mallett	235.50	0	235.50	23.55	14.60	3.41	35		158.93
Tom Jones	110.00	0	110.00	11.00	6.82	1.60			90.59
Totals	$1,251.50	$29.70	$1,281.20	$136.63	$79.43	$18.58	$60.00	$15.00	$971.55

11.2		Pay Rate	Fed Income Tax	Other Taxes	
Shirley James	40		6.25	0.10	FICA	0.062
Liam Foote	40		6.50	0.10	Medicare	0.0145
Dick Reed	40	2	9.90	0.12		
Karen Mallett	30		7.85	0.10		
Tom Jones	20		5.50	0.10		

Employers Tax Expense

FUTA	0.08	$102.50
SUTA	0.05	$64.06

Brandon's Payroll Register
June 15

NAME	EARNINGS			DEDUCTIONS						
11.2	Regular	Overtime	Total Pay	Fed Income Tx	Soc. Sec. Tax	Medicare Tax	Child	United Way	Net Pay
Shirley James	250.00	18.75	268.75	26.88	16.66	3.90	25	5	191.32
Liam Foote	260.00	0	260.00	26.00	16.12	3.77			214.11
Dick Reed	396.00	74.25	470.25	56.43	29.16	6.82		10	367.85
Karen Mallett	219.80	0	219.80	21.98	13.63	3.19	35		146.01
Tom Jones	99.00	0	99.00	9.90	6.14	1.44			81.53
Totals	$1,224.80	$93.00	$1,317.80	$141.19	$81.70	$19.11	$60.00	$15.00	$1,000.80

11.2		Pay Rate	Fed Income Tax	Other Taxes	
Shirley James	40	2	6.25	0.10	FICA	0.062
Liam Foote	40	0	6.50	0.10	Medicare	0.0145
Dick Reed	40	5	9.90	0.12		
Karen Mallett	28		7.85	0.10		
Tom Jones	18		5.50	0.10		

Employers Tax Expense

FUTA	0.08	$105.42
SUTA	0.05	$65.89

Brandon's Payroll Register
June 30

NAME	EARNINGS			DEDUCTIONS						
11.2	Regular	Overtime	Total Pay	Fed Income Tx	Soc. Sec. Tax	Medicare Tax	Child	United Way	Net Pay
Shirley James	250.00	46.88	296.88	29.69	18.41	4.30	25	5	214.48
Liam Foote	260.00	19.5	279.50	27.95	17.33	4.05			230.17
Dick Reed	396.00	118.8	514.80	61.78	31.92	7.46		10	403.64
Karen Mallett	251.20	0	251.20	25.12	15.57	3.64	35		171.86
Tom Jones	203.50	0	203.50	20.35	12.62	2.95			167.58
Totals	$1,360.70	$185.18	$1,545.88	$164.88	$95.84	$22.42	$60.00	$15.00	$1,187.73

11.2		Pay Rate	Fed Income Tax	Other Taxes	
Shirley James	40	5	6.25	0.10	FICA	0.062
Liam Foote	40	2	6.50	0.10	Medicare	0.0145
Dick Reed	40	8	9.90	0.12		
Karen Mallett	32		7.85	0.10		

Employers Tax Expense

FUTA	0.08	$123.67
SUTA	0.05	$77.29

Mike Brandon
11.2 CASH JOURNAL

	CASH		DATE		DESCRIPTION	Post	GENERAL	
	Debit	Credit	Month	Day		Ref	Debit	Credit
1			June	1	Employer Tax Expense 5/15	530	274.29	
2					FICA Taxes Payable	222		82.35
3					Medicare Taxes Payable	225		19.26
4					F U T A Taxes Payable	240		106.26
5					S U T A Taxes Payable	242		66.42
6				1	Wages/Salary Expense	550	1,281.20	
7					^ Federal Income Tax Payable	220		136.64
8					FICA Taxes Payable	222		79.43
9					Medicare Taxes Payable	225		18.58
10					Child Care Payable	230		60.00
11					United Way Payable	232		15.00
12					Cash - Payroll	115		971.55
13		971.55		1	Cash - Payroll	115	971.55	
14				1	Employer Tax Expense	530	264.57	
15					FICA Taxes Payable	222		79.43
16					Medicare Taxes Payable	225		18.58
17					F U T A Taxes Payable	240		102.50
18					S U T A Taxes Payable	242		64.06
19		300.00		3	Rent Expense	535	300.00	
20		500.00		5	Advertising Expense	520	500.00	
21	3,895.00			10	Sales	410		3,895.00
22				11	Purchases	510	5,000.00	
23					Accounts Payable / Lee	210		5,000.00
24				15	Wages/Salary Expense	550	1,317.80	
25					Federal Income Tax Payable	220		141.19
26					FICA Taxes Payable	222		81.70
27					Medicare Taxes Payable	225		19.11
28					Child Care Payable	230		60.00
29					United Way Payable	232		15.00
30					Cash - Payroll	115		1,000.80
31		1,000.80			Cash - Payroll	115	1,000.80	
32					Employer Tax Expense	530	272.12	
33					FICA Taxes Payable	222		81.70
34					Medicare Taxes Payable	225		19.11
35					F U T A Taxes Payable	240		105.42
36					S U T A Taxes Payable	242		65.89

Mike Brandon's Cash Journal page 2

	CASH		DATE		DESCRIPTION	Post	GENERAL	
	Debit	Credit	Month	Day		Ref	Debit	Credit
1	5,384.00		June	16	Sales	410		5,384.00
2		5,000.00		17	Accounts Payable / Lees	210	5,000.00	
3		10,000.00		18	Notes Payable / Lucky Bank	250	10,000.00	
4		500.00		19	Advertising Expense	520	500.00	
5	7,778.00			25	Sales	410		7,778.00
6		250.00		26	Mike Brandon's, Drawing	320	250.00	
7		2,000.00		27	Accounts Payable / Lees	210	2,000.00	
8				30	Wages/Salary Expense	550	1,545.88	
9					^ Federal Income Tax Payable	220		164.89
10					FICA Taxes Payable	222		95.84
11					Medicare Taxes Payable	225		22.42
12					Child Care Payable	230		60.00
13					United Way Payable	232		15.00
14					Cash - Payroll	115		1,187.73
15		1,187.73		30	Cash - Payroll	115	1,187.73	
16				30	Employer Tax Expense	530	319.22	
17					FICA Taxes Payable	222		95.84
18					Medicare Taxes Payable	225		22.42
19					F U T A Taxes Payable	240		123.67
20					S U T A Taxes Payable	242		77.29
21								
22								
23								
24								
25								
26								
27								
28								
29								
30	17,057.00	21,710.08					31,985.16	27,332.08

Prove Cash Journal   Difference   0.00

Debit	Credit
49,042.16	49,042.16

BRANDON'S
TRIAL BALANCE
June 30.......

11.2

	DESCRIPTION	PR	DEBIT	CREDIT
1	Cash		98,418.62	
2	Cash - Payroll		0.00	
3	Office Supplies		200.00	
4	Inventory		100,000.00	
5	Accounts Payable			15,000.00
6	Federal Income Tax Payable			442.72
7	FICA Payable			596.29
8	Medicare Payable			139.48
9	Child Care Payable			240.00
10	United Way Payable			60.00
11	Federal Unemployment Payable			437.85
12	State Unemployment Payable			273.66
13	Notes Payable			80,000.00
14	Mike Brandon, Capital			25,000.00
15	Mike Brandon, Drawing		550.00	
16	Sales			112,832.00
17	Purchases		25,000.00	
18	Advertising Expense		3,500.00	
19	Employer Tax Expense		1,130.20	
20	Rent Expense		600.00	
21	Utility Expense		150.00	
22	Wages & Salary Expense		5,473.18	
23	Total Debits and Credits		$235,022.00	$235,022.00
24				
25				
26				

Mark Edwards Company

12.2 PURCHASES JOURNAL — Page 1

	DATE		Dis	Name of Account	Post Ref	Purchases Debit / Accounts Pay. Credit
1	Mar	7	X	Leonards's Wholesale		9,600
2		11	X	Pierce Arrow Supply		18,900
3		15	X	Beal Brother's Big Bargin Barn		4,220
4						
7						
8	Discount	0.02	0.01			
9	192	9,408				
10	378	18,522				
11	40	3,960				
12						
13						

Tipton's Toy World

12.3 SALES JOURNAL — Page 1

	DATE		Dis	Name of Account	Post Ref	Accounts Rec Debit / Sales Credit
1	April	5	2%	Toys for Kids		5,500
2		9	2%	Kid's Land		10,365
3		17	3or2%	John's 5 & 10		4,450
4						
5	Discount	0.02	0.03			
6	110	5,390				
7	207.30			10,157.70		
8	120.00					
9						

12.2   EDWARDS Company
Cash Journal

Page 1

#	CASH Debit	CASH Credit	Month	Day	DESCRIPTION	Post Ref	GENERAL Debit	GENERAL Credit
1	50,000.00		Mar	5	Mark Edwards, Capital			70,000.00
2					Inventory		20,000.00	
3		1,100.00		8	Rent Expense		1,100.00	
4				12	Office Supplies		129.00	
5					Acc Pay/Central Off Sup			129.00
6	6,985.00			13	Sales			6,985.00
7		9,408.00		14	Acc Pay/Leonard's Wholes		9,600.00	
8					Purchases Discount			192.00
9	7,382.00			20	Sales			9,382.00
10					Accounts Receivable		2,000.00	
11		18,522.00		21	Acc Pay/ Pierce Arrow		18,900.00	
12					Purchases Discount			378.00
13		283.57		22	Utilities Expense		283.57	
14				23	Purchases (Purchases Return)			220.00
15					Acc Pay/Beal Brothers		220.00	
16		3,960.00		24	Acc Pay/Beal Brothers		4,000.00	
17					Purchases Discount			40.00
18				25	Wage Expense		3,778.00	
19					Federal Income Tax Pay			582.00
20					FICA Payable			234.24
21					Medicare Payable			54.28
22					Cash Payroll			2,906.98
23		2,907.48			Cash Payroll		2,906.98	
24				25	Employer Payroll Expense		780.16	
25					FICA Payable			234.24
26					Medicare Payable			54.78
27					FUTA Payable			302.24
28					State Employment Payable			188.90
29	64,367.00	36,181.05					63,697.71	91,883.66
30								
31	Gross Wages	FICA	0.08					
32	3,778.00	234.24	302.24				128,064.71	128,064.71
33	Fed Tax	Med	0.05		Net Wages			
34	582.00	54.78	188.90		$2,906.98			

12.3 Tipton's Toy World Cash Journal

Page 1

	CASH		DATE		DESCRIPTION	Post	GENERAL	
	Debit	Credit	Month	Day		Ref	Debit	Credit
1			April	1	Inventory		75,000.00	
2	20,000.00				Tiption's Capital			95,000.00
3		875.00		6	Rent Expense		875.00	
4	2,254.00			10	Sales			2,254.00
5	5,390.00			12	Acc Rec/Toy's for Kids			5,500.00
6					Sales Discount		110.00	
7				16	Office Supplies		258.00	
8					Accounts Pay/Central Off			258.00
9	10,157.70			18	Acc Rec/Kid's Land			10,365.00
10					Sales Discount		207.30	
11				19	Sales (Sales Returns & Allowances)		450.00	
12					Acc Rec/John's 5 & 10			450.00
13	1,988.00			22	Sales			1,988.00
14		289.00		23	Utilities Expense		289.00	
15	3,880.00			27	Acc Rec/John's 5 & 10			4,000.00
16					Sales Discount		120.00	
17		68.07		28	Office Supplies		23.54	
18					Postage		41.20	
19					Miscellaneous Expense		3.33	
20								
21								
22	43,669.70	1,232.07					77,377.37	119,815.00
23								
24								
25								
26							121,047.07	121,047.07
27								
28								

HART & SON
12.4 - 13.4   ## CASH JOURNAL

Page 1

	CASH		DATE		DESCRIPTION	Post	GENERAL	
	Debit	Credit	Month	Day		Ref	Debit	Credit
1		1,200.00	Nov	3	Rent Expense	525	1,200.00	
2	555.00			7	Sales	410		555.00
3		7,704.76		12	Accounts Pay/Lyle & Son	210/82	7,862.00	
4					Purchases Discount	520		157.24
5		5,000.00		13	Truck	150	27,000.00	
6					Notes Payable	240		22,000.00
7	12,141.22			14	Sales Discount	415	247.78	
8					Accounts Rec/Hill & Daugh	120/71		12,389.00
9		225.00		16	Utility Expense	540	225.00	
10	472.00			17	Cash Sales	410		472.00
11		2,500.00		18	Notes Payable	240	2,500.00	
12				20	Office Equipment	135	2,678.00	
13					Accounts Pay/ACE Supply	210/80		2,678.00
14		4,604.04		21	Accounts Pay/ Lewis	210/81	4,698.00	
15					Purchases Discount	515		93.96
16		6,187.50		24	Accounts Pay/Twin Sisters	210/85	6,250.00	
17					Purchases Discount	515		62.50
18		33.81		25	Office Supplies Expense	560	28.98	
19					Misc Expense	575	4.83	
20		500.00		26	Hart & Sons, Drawing	315	500.00	
21				27	Wage Expense	545	1,343.00	
22					Federal Income Tax Pay	205		98.50
23					FICA Payable	207		114.83
24					Medicare Payable	208		12.18
25					Cash Payroll	115		1,117.49
26		1,117.49			Cash Payroll	115	1,117.49	
27				27	Employer Payroll Expense	530	301.60	
28					FICA Payable	207		114.83
29					Medicare Payable	208		12.18
30					FUTA Payable	220		107.44
31					State Employment Payable	222		67.15
32	13,168.22	29,072.60					55,956.68	40,052.30
33	(110)	(110)					(x)	(X)
34	69,124.90	69,124.90				69,124.90		
35						69,124.90		

HART & SON
CASH JOURNAL

Page 2

	CASH		DATE		DESCRIPTION	Post	GENERAL	
	Debit	Credit	Month	Day		Ref	Debit	Credit
1			Dec	1	Sales Returns & Allowances	420	442.00	
2					Accounts Rec/Woods World	120/72		442.00
3				1	Sales Discount	415	180.06	
4	8,822.94				Accounts Rec/Woods World	120/72		9,003.00
5		1,200.00		3	Rent Expense	525	1,200.00	
6				5	Office Supplies	130	389.00	
7					Accounts Pay/ACE Supply	210/80		389.00
8	739.00			6	Cash Sales	410		739.00
9				9	Accounts Pay/Lewis Bros.	210/81	250.00	
10					Purchases Returns & All	520		250.00
11		1,653.06		12	Accounts Pay/Lewis Bros.	210/81	1,686.80	
12					Purchases Discount	515		33.74
13				13	Sales Returns & Allowances	420	283.00	
14					Accounts Rec/Hill & Daugh	120/71		283.00
15	5,261.76			13	Sales Discount	415	53.15	
16					Accounts Rec/Hill & Daugh	120/71		5,314.91
17				19	Accounts Pay/TwinSisters	210/85	443.00	
18					Purchases Returns & All	520		443.00
19		295.00			Utilities Expense	540	295.00	
20				21	Sales Returns & Allowances	420	214.00	
21					Accounts Rec/Woods World	120/72		214.00
22		500.00		23	Accounts Pay/ACE Supply	210/80	500.00	
23	14,823.70	3,648.06					5,936.01	17,111.65
24	(110)	(110)					(X)	(X)
25								
26	Total Debit	20,759.71						
27	Total Credit	20,759.71						
28								
29								

HART & SONS TRIAL BALANCE
October 31

	DATE		DESCRIPTION	PR	DEBIT	CREDIT
1						
2			Cash		26,568.14	
3			Office Supplies		321.82	
4			Office Equipment		10,863.21	
5			Inventory		8,000.00	
6			Accounts Payable			1,000.00
7			Hart & Son, Capital			44,753.17
8						
9					45,753.17	45,753.17
10						
11						
12						
13						
14						
15						
16						
17						
18						
19						
20						
21						
22						
23						
24						

HART & SONS
PURCHASES JOURNAL

12.4 - 13.4 | Page 3

	DATE		Dis	Name of Account	Post Ref	Purchases Debit Accounts Pay. Credit
1	Nov	2	X	Lyle & Sons	82	7,862
2		11	X	Lewis Brothers	81	4,698
3		15	X	Twin Sisters	85	6,250
4						18,810
7						(510) (210)
8						
9	Dec	2	X	Lewis Brothers		1,936.80
10		14	X	Twin Sisters		2,989.80
11						4,926.60
12						(510) (210)
13						
14						
15						

HART & SONS
SALES JOURNAL

12.4 & 13.4 | Page 5

	DATE		Dis	Name of Account	Post Ref	Accounts Rec Debit Sales Credit
1	Nov	4	X	Hill & Daughter	71	12,389
2		22	X	Woods World	72	9,445
3						21,834
4						(120) (410)
5						
6	Dec	4	X	Hill & Daughter	71	5,597.91
7		15	X	Woods World	72	6,005.12
8		22	X	Hill & Daughter	71	3,006.56
9						14,609.59
10						(120) (410)
11						
12						

12.4 & 13.4

HART & SON
General Journal

Account | **CASH** | No. 110

DATE		ITEM	PR	Debit	Credit	BALANCE Debit	BALANCE Credit
Nov	1	BALANCE		26,568.14		26,568.14	
	30		1	13,168.22	29,072.60	10,663.76	
Dec	30		2	14,823.70	3,648.06	21,839.40	

Account | **CASH - PAYROLL** | No.115

DATE		ITEM	PR	Debit	Credit	BALANCE Debit	BALANCE Credit
Nov	27		1	1,117.49		1,117.49	
					1,117.49	0.00	

Account | **ACCOUNTS RECEIVABLE** | No. 120

DATE		ITEM	PR	Debit	Credit	BALANCE Debit	BALANCE Credit
Nov	14		1		12,389.00		12,389.00
	30		SJ 5	21,834.00		9,445.00	
Dec	1		1		442.00		
	1		1		9,003.00		
	13		2		283.00		
	13		2		5,314.91		
	21		2		214.00		
	30		SJ 5	14,609.59	15,256.91	8,797.68	

ALLOWANCE FOR DOUBTFUL ACCOUNTS   No.125

DATE		ITEM	PR	Debit	Credit	BALANCE Debit	BALANCE Credit
Nov	1	BALANCE			139.24		139.24

Account — **OFFICE SUPPLIES** — No. 130

DATE		ITEM	PR	Debit	Credit	BALANCE Debit	BALANCE Credit
Nov	1	BALANCE				321.82	
Dec	5.00		2	389.00		710.82	

OFFICE EQUIPMENT — No.135

DATE		ITEM	PR	Debit	Credit	BALANCE Debit	BALANCE Credit
Nov	1	BALANCE				10,863.21	
	20		1	2,678.00		13,541.21	

ALLOWANCE FOR DEPRECIATION OFFICE EQUIPMENT — No. 140

DATE		ITEM	PR	Debit	Credit	BALANCE Debit	BALANCE Credit
Jan	1	BALANCE			2,683.21		2,683.21

DELIVERY TRUCK — No. 150

DATE		ITEM	PR	Debit	Credit	BALANCE Debit	BALANCE Credit
Nov	13		1	27,000.00		27,000.00	

ALLOWANCE FOR DEPRECIATION — No. 155

DATE		ITEM	PR	Debit	Credit	BALANCE Debit	BALANCE Credit

Account — **INVENTORY** — No. 160

DATE		ITEM	PR	Debit	Credit	BALANCE Debit	BALANCE Credit
Nov	1	BALANCE				8,000.00	

Account **FEDERAL INCOME TAX PAYABLE** No. 205

DATE		ITEM	PR	Debit	Credit	BALANCE Debit	BALANCE Credit
Nov	27		1		98.50		98.50

Account **FICA PAYABLE** No. 207

DATE		ITEM	PR	Debit	Credit	BALANCE Debit	BALANCE Credit
Nov	27		1		114.83		114.83
			1		114.83		229.66

Account **MEDICARE PAYABLE** No. 208

DATE		ITEM	PR	Debit	Credit	BALANCE Debit	BALANCE Credit
Nov	27		1		12.18		12.18
	27		1		12.18		24.36

Account **ACCOUNTS PAYABLE** No. 210

DATE		ITEM	PR	Debit	Credit	BALANCE Debit	BALANCE Credit
Nov	*1*	*BALANCE*					1,000.00
	12		1	7,862.00		6,862.00	
	20		1		2,678.00	4,184.00	
	21		1	4,698.00			
	24		1	6,250.00			
Nov	30		PJ 3	*10,948.00*	18,810.00		3,678.00
Dec	5		2		389.00		4,067.00
	9		2	250.00			
	12		2	1,686.80			
	19		2	443.00			
	23		2	500.00			
	30		PJ 3	*2,879.80*	4,926.60		6,113.80

Account **FUTA PAYABLE** No. 220

DATE		ITEM	PR	Debit	Credit	BALANCE Debit	BALANCE Credit
Nov	27		1		107.44		107.44

12.4, 13.4 and 15.4 Hart and Son General Ledger page 4

| Account | STATE EMPLOYMENT PAYABLE | | | | No. 222 | | |

DATE		ITEM	PR	Debit	Credit	BALANCE Debit	BALANCE Credit
Nov	27		1		67.15		67.15

| Account | INTEREST PAYABLE | | | | No. 225 | | |

DATE		ITEM	PR	Debit	Credit	BALANCE Debit	BALANCE Credit

| Account | WAGES PAYABLE | | | | No. 230 | | |

DATE		ITEM	PR	Debit	Credit	BALANCE Debit	BALANCE Credit

| Account | NOTES PAYABLE | | | | No. 240 | | |

DATE		ITEM	PR	Debit	Credit	BALANCE Debit	BALANCE Credit
Nov	13		1		22,000.00		22,000.00
Nov	18		1	2,500.00			19,500.00

| Account | HART & SONS, CAPITAL | | | | No. 310 | | |

DATE		ITEM	PR	Debit	Credit	BALANCE Debit	BALANCE Credit
Nov	1	BALANCE					41,930.72

| Account | HART & SONS, DRAWING | | | | No.315 | | |

DATE		ITEM	PR	Debit	Credit	BALANCE Debit	BALANCE Credit
Nov	26		1	500.00		500.00	

Account INCOME SUMMARY No. 330

DATE	ITEM	PR	Debit	Credit	BALANCE Debit	BALANCE Credit

Account SALES No. 410

DATE		ITEM	PR	Debit	Credit	BALANCE Debit	BALANCE Credit
Nov	7		1		555.00		555.00
	17		1		472.00		1,027.00
	30		SJ 5		21,834.00		22,861.00
Dec	6		2		739.00		23,600.00
	30		SJ 5		14,609.59		38,209.59

Account SALES DISCOUNT No. 415

DATE		ITEM	PR	Debit	Credit	BALANCE Debit	BALANCE Credit
Nov	14		1	247.78		247.78	
Dec	1		2	180.06		427.84	
	13		2	53.15		480.99	

Account SALES RETURNS & ALLOWANCES No. 420

DATE		ITEM	PR	Debit	Credit	BALANCE Debit	BALANCE Credit
Dec	1		2	442.00		442.00	
	13		2	283.00		725.00	
	21		2	214.00		939.00	

Account PURCHASES No. 510

DATE		ITEM	PR	Debit	Credit	BALANCE Debit	BALANCE Credit
Nov	30		PJ 3	18,810.00		18,810.00	
Dec	30		PJ 3	4,926.60		23,736.60	

Account PURCHASES DISCOUNT No. 515

DATE		ITEM	PR	Debit	Credit	BALANCE Debit	BALANCE Credit
Nov	12		1		157.24		157.24
	21		1		93.96		251.20
	24		1		62.50		313.70
	12		2		33.74		347.44

Account PURCHASES RETURNS & ALLOWANCES No. 520

DATE		ITEM	PR	Debit	Credit	BALANCE Debit	BALANCE Credit
Dec	9		2		250.00		250.00
	19		2		443.00		693.00

Account RENT EXPENSE No. 525

DATE		ITEM	PR	Debit	Credit	BALANCE Debit	BALANCE Credit
Nov	3		1	1,200.00		1,200.00	
Dec	3		2	1,200.00		2,400.00	

Account EMPLOYER PAYROLL EXPENSE No. 530

DATE		ITEM	PR	Debit	Credit	BALANCE Debit	BALANCE Credit
Nov	27		1	301.60		301.60	

Account DOUBTFUL ACCOUNTS EXPENSE No. 535

DATE		ITEM	PR	Debit	Credit	BALANCE Debit	BALANCE Credit

Account   **UTILITIES EXPENSE**   No. 540

DATE		ITEM	PR	Debit	Credit	BALANCE Debit	Credit
Nov	16		1	225.00		225.00	
	20		2	295.00		520.00	

Account   **WAGE EXPENSE**   No. 545

DATE		ITEM	PR	Debit	Credit	BALANCE Debit	Credit
Nov	27		1	1,343.00		1,343.00	

Account   **DEPRECIAITON EXPENSE**   No. 555

DATE		ITEM	PR	Debit	Credit	BALANCE Debit	Credit

Account   **OFFICE SUPPLIES EXPENSE**   No. 560

DATE		ITEM	PR	Debit	Credit	BALANCE Debit	Credit
Nov	25		1	28.98		28.98	

Account   **MISCELLANEOUS EXPENSE**   No. 575

DATE		ITEM	PR	Debit	Credit	BALANCE Debit	Credit
Nov	25		1	4.83		4.83	

12.4 - 13.4　　　　　　　**HART & SONS**

ACCOUNTS RECEIVABLE LEDGER

Company Name **HILL & DAUGHTER**　　　　　　　　　　Account # 71

DATE		ITEM	Post	TRIAL BALANCE		DEBIT
Month	Day		Ref	Debit	Credit	Balance
Nov	4		SJ 5	12,389.00		12,389.00
	14		CJ 1		12,389.00	0.00
Dec	4		SJ 5	5,597.91		5,597.91
	13		2		283.00	
	13		2		5,314.91	0.00
	22		SJ 5	3,006.56		3,006.56

Company Name **WOODS WORLD**　　　　　　　　　　Account # 72

DATE		ITEM	Post	TRIAL BALANCE		DEBIT
Month	Day		Ref	Debit	Credit	Balance
Nov	22		SJ 5	9,445.00		9,445.00
Dec	1		2		442.00	
	1		2		9,003.00	0.00
	15		SJ 5	6,005.12		6,005.12
	21		2		214.00	5,791.12

HART & SONS

SCHEDULE OF ACCOUNTS RECEIVABLE

Act #	NAME	AMOUNT
71	Hill & Daughter	3,006.56
72	Woods World	5,791.12
	Total	$8,797.68

HART & SONS

SCHEDULE OF ACCOUNTS PAYABLE

Act #	NAME	AMOUNT
80	ACE SUPPLY	3,567.00
85	Twin Sisters	2,546.80
		$6,113.80

12.4 - 13.4 **HART & SONS**
ACCOUNTS PAYABLE LEDGER

Company Name **ACE SUPPLY**   Account # 80

DATE		ITEM	Post	TRIAL BALANCE		CREDIT
Month	Day		Ref	Debit	Credit	Balance
NOV	1	Balance	X			1,000.00
Nov	19		1		2,678.00	3,678.00
Dec	5		2		389.00	4,067.00
	23		2	500.00		3,567.00

Company Name **LEWIS BROTHERS**   Account # 81

DATE		ITEM	Post	TRIAL BALANCE		CREDIT
Month	Day		Ref	Debit	Credit	Balance
Nov	11		PJ 3		4,698.00	4,698.00
	20		1	4,698.00		0.00
Dec	2		PJ 3		1,936.80	
	9		2	250.00		
	12		2	1,686.80		0.00

Company Name **LYLE & SONS**   Account # 82

DATE		ITEM	Post	TRIAL BALANCE		CREDIT
Month	Day		Ref	Debit	Credit	Balance
Nov	2		PJ 3		7,862.00	7,862.00
	12		CJ 1	7,862.00		0.00

Company Name **TWIN SISTERS**   Account # 85

DATE		ITEM	Post	TRIAL BALANCE		CREDIT
Month	Day		Ref	Debit	Credit	Balance
Nov	15		PJ 3		6,250.00	6,250.00
	24		CJ 1	6,250.00		0.00
Dec	14		PJ 3		2,989.80	
	19		2	443.00		2,546.80

13.1	List Price	Trade Discount		Quanity Discount		Purchased	Selling Price
1	250	0.2	0.1	Yes 20	0.1	35	$162.00
2	340	0.25	0.3333	Yes 50	0.1	60	$153.01
3	425	0.2	0.2	No 40		25	$272.00
4	180	0.1	0.1	no 25		11	$145.80
5	680	0.25	0.2	Yes 20	0.01	30	$403.92

13.2	List Price	Trade Discount		Quanity Discount		Purchased	Selling Price
1	$7,990.00	0.2	0.1				$5,752.80
2	$3,600.00	0.1	0.1				$2,916.00
3	$12,400.00	0.1	0.33333		0.1		$6,696.03
4							

13.3	List Price	Trade Discount		Quanity Discount		Purchased	Selling Price
1	$9,500.00	0.25	0.1				$6,412.50
2	$7,329.00	0.2	0.1				$5,276.88
3	$3,400.00	0.15	0.1		0.05		$2,470.95
21	100.00	0.15	0.1		0.05		72.6750
22	1.00	0.15	0.1		0.05		0.726750
23							
24							

13.4	List Price	Trade Discount		Quanity Discount		Purchased	Selling Price
1	$2,690.00	0.2	0.1				$1,936.80
2	$6,911.00	0.1	0.1				$5,597.91
3	$4,983.00	0.25	0.2				$2,989.80
4	$9,383.00	0.2	0.2				$6,005.12
5	$3,956.00	0.2	0.05				$3,006.56

Reynold's INC
CASH JOURNAL
Page __1

	CASH		DATE		DESCRIPTION	Post	GENERAL	
	Debit	Credit	Month	Day		Ref	Debit	Credit
1		1,300.00	June	1	Rent		1,300.00	
2				2	Accounts Receivable/JB H.		5,752.80	
3					Sales			5,752.80
4				5	Accounts Receivable/ ABC		2,916.00	
5					Sales			2,916.00
6	2,500.00			8	Sales			2,500.00
7				9	Sales Returns & Allowances		500.00	
8					Acc. Rec./J.B. Hilltop			500.00
9		600.00		10	Utilities		600.00	
10	5,147.74			12	Acc. Rec./J.B. Hilltop			5,252.80
11					Sales Discount		105.06	
12				13	Accounts Rec./Paper sup		6,696.00	
13					Sales			6,696.00
14	2,857.68			14	Acc. Rec./A.B.See			2,916.00
15					Sales Discount		58.32	
16				20	Sales Returns & Allowances		1,200.00	
17					Acc Rec../ Paper Sup			1,200.00
18	5,386.08			21	Acc. Rec / Paper supply			5,496.00
19					Sales Discount		109.92	
21		39.75		25	Office Supplies		32.50	
22					Postage		4.50	
23					Misc. Expenses		2.75	
24								
25	15,891.50	1,939.75					19,277.85	33,229.60
25								
26								
27								
28								
29								
30								

Roller, INC
13.3 CASH JOURNAL
Page__1

	CASH		DATE		DESCRIPTION	Post	GENERAL	
	Debit	Credit	Month	Day		Ref	Debit	Credit
1			July	1	Truck		16,000.00	
2		6,000.00			Note Payable			10,000.00
3				2	Purchases		6,412.50	
4					Accounts Pay/Oscar			6,412.50
5				6	Accounts Receivable		10,000.00	
6					Sales			10,000.00
7				7	Purchases		5,276.88	
8					Accounts Pay/Joe's			5,276.88
9		495.00		8	Utilities Expense		495.00	
10				10	Accounts Pay/Oscar		350.00	
11					Purchases Returns & All			350.00
12		5,941.25		12	Accounts Pay/ Oscar's		6,062.50	
13					Purchases Discount			121.25
14				15	Purchases		2,470.95	
15					Accounts Pay/Karen's			2,470.95
16		5,171.34		17	Accounts Pay/Joe's		5,276.88	
17					Purchases Discount			105.54
18				18	Accounts Pay/Karen's		100.00	
19					Purchases Returns & All			100.00
21				25	Accounts Receivable		13,000.00	
22					Sales			13,000.00
23		2,370.95		28	Accounts Pay/Karen's		2,370.95	
24		500.00		29	Roller, Drawing		500.00	
25								
25		20,478.54			68,315.66		68,315.66	47,837.12
26								

13.4 14.4 Hart and Son Trial Balance

Problem #_14.4

Company **HART & SONS**

Worksheet

Date

	ACCOUNT	TRIAL BALANCE		ADJUSTMENTS COLUMN		E - INCOME STATEMENT - I		A - BALANCE SHEET - L & C	
		Debit	Credit	Debit	Credit	Debit	Credit	Debit	Credit
1	Cash	21,839.40							
2	Accounts Receivable	8,797.68							
3	Allow Doubt Accounts		139.24						
4	Office Supplies	710.82							
5	Office Equipment	13,541.21							
6	Allow. for Dep. Off Eq		2,683.21						
7	Delivery Truck	27,000.00							
8	Allow for Dep Del Eq								
9	Inventory	8,000.00							
10	Federal Income Tax Pay		98.50						
11	FICA Payable		229.66						
12	Medicare Pay		24.36						
13	Accounts Payable		6,113.80						
14	FUTA Payable		107.44						
15	State Emp Payable		67.15						
16	Interest Payable								
17	Wages Payable								
19	Notes Payable		19,500.00						
20	Hart & Sons, Capital		41,930.72						
21	Hart & Sons, Drawing	500.00							
22	Income Summary								
23	Sales		38,209.59						
24	Sales Discount	480.99							
25	Sales Returns & Allow.	939.00							
26	Purchases	23,736.60							
27	Purchases Discount		347.44						
28	Purchases Ret. & Allow		693.00						
29	Rent Expense	2,400.00							
30	Employer Payroll Ex	301.60							
31	Bad Debts Expense								
32	Utilities Expense	520.00							
33	Wage Expense	1,343.00							
34	Depreciation Expense								
35	Office Supplies Expense	28.98							
36	Interest Expense								
37	Miscellaneous Expense	4.83							
38		110,144.11	110,144.11						
39									
40									
41									
42									
43									
44									
45									
46				21,749.30	21,749.30	39,850.03	39,850.03	80,607.29	80,607.29

14.1   Tittle Title

GENERAL JOURNAL

Page_1

DATE		DESCRIPTION	PR	DEBIT	CREDIT
		Adusting Entries			
435	1	Supplies Expense		348.00	
87		Office Supplies			348.00
	2	Insurance Expense		135.00	
		PrePaid Insurance			135.00
181	3	Postage Expense		148.00	
33		Postage			148.00
143600	4	Bad Debts Expense	0.01	1,175.00	
261		Allowance for Bad Debts			1,175.00
	5	Income Summary		8,628.00	
		Inventory (Old)			8,628.00
	5	Inventory (New)		9,863.00	
		Income Summary			9,863.00

14.3   Adjustments for Accounts Receivable   1%   Balance $320,688.00

	1	Bad Debts Expense		$3,021.88	
$185 cr		Allowance for Bad Debts			3,021.88
		Bad Debts Expense		3,206.88	
$0		Allowance for Bad Debts			3,206.88
		Bad Debts Expense		3,292.88	
$86 dr		Allowance for Bad Debts			3,292.88

Q. D. Shanks Lumber Yard
Inventory Assessment

14.2

#1	Average	LIFO	FIFO
Hammers	$55.23	$86.70	$43.00

	Number	Price	Total
Beginning	15	8.67	$130.05
Purchase #1	25	5.83	$145.75
Purchase #2	50	4.50	$225.00
Purchase #3	20	5.95	$119.00
Purchase #4	10	4.30	$43.00
120			
Ending Inven	10		662.8

#2	Average	LIFO	FIFO
Sander	$1,860.42	$1,750.00	$1,965.00

	Number	Price	Total
Beginning	5	350.00	$1,750.00
Purchase #1	2	375.00	$750.00
Purchase #2	1	425.00	$425.00
Purchase #3	2	375.00	$750.00
Purchase #4	2	395.00	$790.00
12			
Ending Inven	5		$4,465.00

#3	Average	LIFO	FIFO
18' Pine	$13,539.71	$13,900.00	$14,600.00

	Number	Price	Total
Beginning	400	16.00	$6,400.00
Purchase #1	500	15.00	$7,500.00
Purchase #2	1,000	14.25	$14,250.00
Purchase #3	1,000	14.00	$14,000.00
Purchase #4	500	18.00	$9,000.00
3,400			
Ending Inven	900		$51,150.00

#4	Average	LIFO	FIFO
4X8 Sheets	$1,132.00	$1,110.00	$1,250.00

	Number	Price	Total
Beginning	200	2.25	$450.00
Purchase #1	300	2.20	$660.00
Purchase #2	500	2.00	$1,000.00
Purchase #3	500	2.10	$1,050.00
Purchase #4	1,000	2.50	$2,500.00
2,500			
Ending Inven	500		$5,660.00

#5	Average	LIFO	FIFO
3" Nails	$284.12	$310.00	$270.00

	#lbs	Price	Total
Beginning	100	1.00	$100.00
Purchase #1	100	1.10	$110.00
Purchase #2	500	1.00	$500.00
Purchase #3	1,000	0.90	$900.00
Purchase #4			$0.00
1,700			
Ending Inven	300		$1,610.00

14.4. Hart & Son

HART & SONS
Worksheet
Date

	ACCOUNT	TRIAL BALANCE Debit	Credit	ADJUSTMENTS Debit	Credit	E - INCOME STATEMENT - I Debit	Credit	A - BALANCE SHEET - L & C Debit	Credit
1	Cash	21,839.40							
2	Accounts Receivable	8,797.68							
3	Allow Doubt Accounts		139.24						
4	Office Supplies	710.82							
5	Office Equipment	13,541.21							
6	Allow. for Dep. Off Eq		2,683.21						
7	Delivery Truck	27,000.00							
8	Allow for Dep Del Eq								
9	Inventory	8,000.00							
10	Fed Income Tax Pay		98.50						
11	FICA Payable		229.66						
12	Medicare Pay		24.36						
13	Accounts Payable		6,113.80						
14	FUTA Payable		107.44						
15	State Emp Payable		67.15						
16	Interest Payable								
17	Wages Payable								
18	Notes Payable		19,500.00						
19	Hart & Sons, Capital		41,930.72						
20	Hart & Sons, Drawing	500.00							
21	Income Summary								
22	Sales		38,209.59						
23	Sales Discount	480.99							
24	Sales Returns & Allow.	939.00							
25	Purchases	23,736.60							
26	Purchases Discount		347.44						
27	Purchases Ret. & Allow		693.00						
28	Rent Expense	2,400.00							
29	Employer Payroll Ex	301.60							
30	Bad Debts Expense								
31	Utilities Expense	520.00							
32	Wage Expense	1,343.00							
33	Depreciation Expense								
34	Office Supplies Expens	28.98							
35	Interest Expense								
36	Miscellaneous Expense	4.83							
37		110,144.11	110,144.11						
38									
39									
40									
41									
42									
43								34,904.30	39,850.03	80,607.29	75,661.56
44							4,945.73			4,945.73
45				$21,749.30	$21,749.30	$39,850.03	$39,850.03	$80,607.29	$80,607.29

14.4 Hart & Son Worksheet

HART & SONS

Worksheet

DATE

	ACCOUNT	TRIAL BALANCE		ADJUSTMENTS COLUMN		E - INCOME STATEMENT -		A - BALANCE SHEET - L & C	
		Debit	Credit	Debit	Credit	Debit	Credit	Debit	Credit
1	Cash	21,839.40						21,839.40	
2	Accounts Receivable	8,797.68						8,797.68	
3	Allow. for Doubtful Account		139.24		740.53				879.77
4	Office Supplies	710.82			381.82			329.00	
5	Office Equipment	13,541.21						13,541.21	
6	Allowance for Dep. Off Equip.		2,683.21		1,343.00				4,026.21
7	Delivery Truck	27,000.00						27,000.00	
8	Allowance for Dep. Del. Equip.				1,000.00				1,000.00
9	Inventory	8,000.00		8,600.00	8,000.00			8,600.00	
10	Federal Income Tax Pay		98.50						98.50
11	FICA Payable		229.66						229.66
12	Medicare Payable		24.36						24.36
13	Accounts Payable		6,113.80						6,113.80
14	FUTA Payable		107.44						107.44
15	State Employment Payable		67.15						67.15
16	Interest Payable				187.45				187.45
17	Wages Payable				1,496.50				1,496.50
18	Notes Payable		19,500.00						19,500.00
19	Hart & Sons, Capital		41,930.72						41,930.72
20	Hart & Sons, Drawing	500.00						500.00	
21	Income Summary			8,000.00	8,600.00		600.00		
22	Sales		38,209.59				38,209.59		
23	Sales Discount	480.99				480.99			
24	Sales Returns and Allowances	939.00				939.00			
25	Purchases	23,736.60				23,736.60			
26	Purchases Discount		347.44				347.44		
27	Purchases Returns & Allowance		693.00				693.00		
28	Rent Expense	2,400.00				2,400.00			
29	Employer Payroll Expense	301.60				301.60			
30	Bad Debts Expense			740.53		740.53			
31	Utilities Expense	520.00				520.00			
32	Wage Expense	1,343.00		1,496.50		2,839.50			
33	Depreciation Expense			2,343.00		2,343.00			
34	Office Supplies Expense	28.98		381.82		410.80			
35	Interest Expense			187.45		187.45			
36	Miscellaneous Expenses	4.83				4.83			
37	Total	110,144.11	110,144.11	21,749.30	21,749.30	34,904.30	39,850.03	80,607.29	75,661.56
38							4,945.73		4,945.73
39						39,850.03	39,850.03	80,607.29	80,607.29
40									

15.1 Calculations

Book Value of these Assets at the end of 3 years

15.1

	Orginal Cost	# Yrs	Scrap Valu	Rate		Straight line	Straight Line Scrap Value	Double Declining
A	22,000	5	2,000	20%		8,800.00	8,000.00	4,752.00
B	180,000	15	20,000	15%		144,000.00	128,000.00	61,740.00
C	130,000	10	10,000	25%		91,000.00	84,000.00	16,250.00
D	2,145	7	345	10%		1,225.71	1,028.57	1,098.24
E	84,000	8	4,000	5%		52,500.00	50,000.00	61,236.00

Straight line **NO** Scrap Value considered

A	Orginal Cost	Years	Dep/Year	Book Value
1	22,000	5	4,400	17,600
2	17,600			13,200
3	13,200			8,800

Example: $22,000 / 5 = $4,400 per year
$22,000 - $4,400 = $17,600 BV after 1 year

B	Orginal Cost	Years	Dep/Year	Book Value
1	180,000	15	12,000	168,000
2	168,000			156,000
3	156,000			144,000

C	Orginal Cost	Years	Dep/Year	Book Value
1	130,000	10	13,000	117,000
2	117,000			104,000
3	104,000			91,000

D	Orginal Cost	Years	Dep/Year	Book Value
1	2,145	7	306.43	1,838.57
2	1,838.57			1,532.14
3	1,532.14			1,225.71

E	Orginal Cost	Years	Dep/Year	Book Value
1	84,000	8	10,500	73,500
2	73,500			63,000
3	63,000			52,500

Straight line with Scrap Value considered

A	Orginal Cost	Years	Dep/Year	Book Value
1	22,000	5	4,000	18,000
2	18,000			14,000
3	14,000			10,000

Example: $22,000 - $2,000 = $20,000 to depreciate
$20,000 / 5 = $4,000 $22,000 - $4000 = $18,000 BV

B	Orginal Cost	Years	Dep/Year	Book Value
1	180,000	15	10,667	169,333
2	169,333			158,667
3	158,667			148,000

C	Orginal Cost	Years	Dep/Year	Book Value
1	130,000	10	12,000	118,000
2	118,000			106,000
3	106,000			94,000

D	Orginal Cost	Years	Dep/Year	Book Value
1	2,145	7	257.14	1,887.86
2	1,887.86			1,630.71
3	1,630.71			1,373.57

E	Orginal Cost	Years	Dep/Year	Book Value
1	84,000	8	10,000	74,000
2	74,000			64,000
3	64,000			54,000

Rates used for Double Declining Balance

	1 Rate	Double %	Recipical %	Recipical	Orginal Cos	End of 3yrs
A	20%	40	60	0.216	22,000	4,752.00
B	15%	30	70	0.343	180,000	61,740.00
C	25%	50	50	0.125	130,000	16,250.00
D	10%	20	80	0.512	2,145	1,098.24
E	5%	10	90	0.729	84,000	61,236.00

15.2 Sparks Brothers Calculations and General Journal
15.3 Delivery Truck Depreciation

Sparks Brothers Spray Painting

15.2

CALCULATIONS

	Orginal Cost	Scrap Value	# Years	Year
X	22000	1000	5	2

	Orginal Cost	Amt to Dep	Amt/Year
X	22000	21000	4200

	Orginal Cost	Scrap Value	# Years	Year
Y	32000	2,000	dd 20%	5

	Orginal Cost	Amt to Dep	Amt/Year
Y	32,000.00	30,000.00	
1	30,000.00	12,000.00	18,000.00
	18,000.00	7,200.00	10,800.00
	10,800.00	4,320.00	6,480.00
	6,480.00	2,592.00	3,888.00
	3,888.00	1,555.20	2,332.80

	Orginal Cost	Scrap Value	# Years	Year
Z	110,000	0	10	3

	Orginal Cost	Amt to Dep	Amt/Year
Z	110,000	110,000	11,000

GENERAL JOURNAL

	ACCOUNTS	DEBIT	CREDIT
	Adjusting Entries		
X	Depreciation Expense	4,200.00	
	Allowance Depreciation		4,200.00
Y	Depreciation Expense	1,555.20	
	Allowance Depreciation		1,555.20
Z	Depreciation Expense	11,000.00	
	Allowance Depreciation		11,000.00

15.3

Delivery Truck Depreciation

DT	Orginal Cost	Scrap Value	# Years	Year	D	Orginal Cc	Scrap Value	#	Year
	26,000	6,000	4			28,000	8,000		5

	Orginal Cost	Amt to Dep	Amt/Year			Orginal Cc	Amt to Dep	Amt/Year	
	26,000	20,000	5,000			28,000	20,000		4,000

Computer Depreciation

Cor	Orginal Cost	Scrap Value	# Years	Year	C	Orginal Cc	Scrap Value	#	Year
	4,200	0	7			8,000	1,000		7

	Orginal Cost	Amt to Dep	Amt/Year			Orginal Cc	Amt to Dep	Amt/Year	
	4,200	4,200	600			8,000	7,000		1,000

Cooling Equipment Depreciation

CE	Orginal Cost	Scrap Value	# Years	Year	C	Orginal Cc	Scrap Value	#	Year
	1,500	300	6		E	5,350	450		7

	Orginal Cost	Amt to Dep	Amt/Year			Orginal Cc	Amt to Dep	Amt/Year	
	1,500	1,200	200			5,350	4,900		700

MARY FOXX
CASH JOURNAL

15.3

Page 1

	CASH		DATE		DESCRIPTION	Post	GENERAL	
	Debit	Credit	Month	Day		Ref	Debit	Credit
1				98				
2		26,000.00	Jan	1	Delivery Truck		26,000.00	
3		4,200.00	April	1	Computer/Office Equipment		4,200.00	
4		1,500.00	July	1	Cooling Equipment		1,500.00	
5			Dec	31	Depreciation Expense		5,550.00	
6			1.00	yr	Allow for Dep. Truck			5,000.00
7			0.75		Allow for Dep. Comp.			450.00
8			0.50		Allow for Dep.Cooling EQ			100.00
9			April	1	Depreciation Expense	99	50.00	
10					Allow for Dep. Cooling EQ			50.00
11				1	Cooling Equipment (new)		5,350.00	
12					Allow for Dep. Cooling EQ		150.00	
13		4,000.00			Cooling Equipment (old)			1,500.00
14			Dec	31	Depreciation Expense		6,125.00	
15			1.00	yr	Allow for Dep. Truck			5,000.00
16			1.00		Allow for Dep. Comp.			600.00
17			0.75		Allow for Dep. Cooling EQ			525.00
18			Dec	31	Allow for Dep. Comp.		1,050.00	
19					Loss on Comp. Donation		3,150.00	
20					Computer/Off Equipment			4,200.00
21		8,000.00	Jan	1	Computer/Office Equipment	2000	8,000.00	
22			Mar	17	Depreciation Expense		1,250.00	
23			0.25		Allow for Dep. Truck			1,250.00
24			Mar	17	New Truck		28,000.00	
25					Allow. For Dep Truck (old)		11,250.00	
26		16,000.00			Loss on Trade-In Del Truck		2,750.00	
27					Delivery Truck			26,000.00
28			Dec	31	Depreciation Expense		4,700.00	
29					Allow for Dep. Truck			3,000.00
30					Allow for Dep. Comp.			1,000.00
31					Allow for Dep. Cooling EQ			700.00
32								
33								
		59,700					109,075	
							109,075	49,375

HART & SONS
Income Statement
For the Month of December

15.4 (12.4,13.4,14.4)

DESCRIPTION	PR	DEBIT	CREDIT
Sales		38,209.59	
Less Sales Discount		-480.99	
Sales Returns and Allowances		-939.00	
Gross Sales			36,789.60
Cost of Good Sold			
Beginning Inventory		8,000.00	
Plus Purchases		23,736.60	
Less Purchases Discount		-347.44	
Purchases Returns and Allowances		-693.00	
Merchandise Available for Sale		30,696.16	
Less Ending Inventory		-8,600.00	
Cost of Good Sold			22,096.16
Gross Income from Sales			14,693.44
Operating Expenses			
Rent Expense		2,400.00	
Employer Payroll Expense		301.60	
Bat Debts Expense		740.53	
Utilities Expense		520.00	
Wage Expense		2,839.50	
Depreciation Exepense		2,343.00	
Office Supplies Expense		410.80	
Miscellaneous Expense		4.83	
Total Operating Expenses			9,560.26
Gross Income			5,133.18
Other Expenses			
Interest Expense			187.45
Net Income			$4,945.73

HART & SONS

Capital Statement

December 31,----------

Beginning Capital			41,930.72
Net Income		4,945.73	
Less Drawing		500.00	
Change in Capital			4,445.73
Capial October 31, 1999			$46,376.45

HART & SONS

Balance Sheet

December 31,------

Assets			
Cash		21,839.40	
Accounts Receivable	8,797.68		
Allowance of Doubtful Accouns	879.77	7,917.91	
Office Supplies		329.00	
Office Equipment	13,541.21		
Allowance of Depreciation Office Eq.	4,026.21	9,515.00	
Delivery Truck	27,000.00		
Allowance for Depreciation	1,000.00	26,000.00	
Inventory		8,600.00	
			$74,201.31
Liabilities			
Federal income Tax Payale		98.50	
FICA Payable		229.66	
Medicare Payable		24.36	
Accounts Payable		6,113.80	
FUTA Payable		107.44	
State Employment Payable		67.15	
Interest Payable		187.45	
Wages Payable		1,496.50	
Notes Payable		19,500.00	
Total Liabilities			27,824.86
Capital			
Hart & Sons, Capital			46,376.45
Total Capital and Liabilities			$74,201.31

CALCULATIONS

	Name	Prinicpal	Rate	Date	Time	
1	Mike Bird	10,000	6%	9/1/1999	4	
2	Tim Ross	16,000	8%	7/1/1999	6	
3	Harold McFall	6,000	5%	5/1/1999	8	
4	Paul Cloyd	12,000	7%	2/1/1999	11	
5	Terri Davis	8,000	10%	3/11/1998	12	

GENERAL JOURNAL

	Accounts	Debit	Credit
	Adjusting Entries		
1	Interest Expense	200.00	
	Interest Payable		200.00
2	Interest Expense	640.00	
	Interest Payable		640.00
3	Interest Expense	200.00	
	Interest Payable		200.00
4	Interest Expense	770.00	
	Interest Payable		770.00
5	Interest Expense	800.00	
	Interest Payable		800.00

2,610.00

The interest on the above notes uses the P x R x T to determine the interst.

The adjusting entry may be a series of debits to Interest Expense and a credit to Interest Payable as shown above.

If the Notes are not kept separate by date, bank, company, or some other classification, one debit to Interest Expense and one credit to Interest Payable for the total can be used.

All Interest Expense accounts are closed in to the Income Summary.

Reversing Entry is the opposite of the Adjusting Entry.

GENERAL JOURNAL

Accounts	Debit	Credit
Adjusting Entries		
Interest Expense	2,610.00	
Interest Payable		2,610.00
Closing Entry		
Income Summary	2,610.00	
Interest Expense		2,610.00
Reversing Entries		
Interest Payable	2,610.00	
Interest Expense		2,610.00

16.2 Lane's Luxury Limousine Service

CALCULATIONS

A. | Wages per Week | #Days | Expense |
|---|---|---|
| $2,500 | 3 | $1,500 |

	Name	Prinicpal	Rate	Date	Time
B	M. Jones	2,000	8%	8/1/2000	5
	S. Reed	5,000	6%	4/1/2000	9
C	Fast Cash	2,000	15%	6/1/2000	7
	Limo Loan	20,000	7%	2/1/2000	11

GENERAL JOURNAL

	Accounts	Debit	Credit
	Adjusting Entries		
1	Wage Expense	1,500.00	
	Wages Payable		1,500.00
2	Interest Receivable	66.67	
	Interest Income		66.67
3	Interest Receivable	225.00	
	Interest Income		225.00
4	Interest Expense	175.00	
	Interest Payable		175.00
5	Interest Expense	1,283.33	
	Interest Payable		1,283.33
		3,250.00	3,250.00

GENERAL JOURNAL

Accounts	Debit	Credit
Adjusting Entries		
Wage Expense	1,500.00	
Wages Payable		1,500.00
Interest Receivable	291.67	
Interest Income		291.67
Interest Expense	1,458.33	
Interest Payable		1,458.33
Closing Entries		
Interest Income	291.67	
Income Summary		291.67
Income Summary	2,958.33	
Wage Expense		1,500.00
Interest Expense		1,458.33
Reversing Entries		
Wage Payable	1,500.00	
Wages Expense		1,500.00
Interst Income	291.67	
Interest Receive		291.67
Interest Payable	1,458.33	
Interest Expense		1,458.33
	9,750.00	9,750.00

The total of Interest Income and Interest Expense are used to record the accrued asset and liabilility.

The Interest Income and Interest Expense accounts are closed into the Income Summary account.

The Reversing Entries are opposite of the Adjusting Entries. These will close the accrued account and place a contra-amount in the income or expense account

MOLLY ELOISE MATERIALS

16.3

Worksheet

December 31,---------

ACCOUNT	TRIAL BALANCE		ADJUSTMENTS COLUMN		E - INCOME STATEMENT - I		A - BALANCE SHEET - L & C	
	Debit	Credit	Debit	Credit	Debit	Credit	Debit	Credit
1 Cash	33,673.21						33,673.21	
2 Accounts Receivable	35,385.13						35,385.13	
3 Allow Doubt Accounts		28.50		679.20				707.70
4 Office Supplies	1,863.48			909.56			953.92	
5 Store Selling Supplies	1,258.65			474.18			784.47	
6 Shipping Supplies	183.22			84.92			98.30	
7 Postage	110.00			53.07			56.93	
8 Pre Paid Insur. Office	2,421.55			1,564.00			857.55	
9 Pre Paid Insur. Truck	1,843.00			921.50			921.50	
10 Office Equipment	25,681.29						25,681.29	
11 Allow. for Dep. Off Eq		10,338.25		5,381.00				15,719.25
12 Delivery Truck	40,365.00						40,365.00	
13 Allow for Dep Del Eq		14,200.00		7,100.00				21,300.00
14 Inventory	15,698.56		12,128.31	15,698.56			12,128.31	
15 Federal Income Tax Pay		3,851.87						3,851.87
16 FICA Payable		1,764.10						1,764.10
17 Medicare Pay		185.43						185.43
18 Accounts Payable		8,879.62						8,879.62
19 FUTA Payable		2,461.76						2,461.76
20 State Emp Payable		1,527.91						1,527.91
21 Interest Payable				228.16				228.16
22 Wages Payable				924.36				924.36
23 Notes Payable		25,831.60						25,831.60
24 Hart & Sons, Capital		31,069.39						31,069.39
25 Hart & Sons, Drawing	3,385.00						3,385.00	
26 Income Summary			15,698.56	12,128.31	3,570.25			
27 Sales		153,735.06				153,735.06		
28 Sales Discount	2,538.16				2,538.16			
29 Sales Returns & Allow.	4,147.75				4,147.75			
30 Purchases	46,315.43				46,315.43			
31 Purchases Discount		2,189.51				2,189.51		
32 Purchases Ret. & Allow		3,392.08				3,392.08		
33 Rent Expense	8,600.00				8,600.00			
34 Employer Payroll Ex	2,384.54				2,384.54			
35 Bad Debts Expense			679.20		679.20			
36 Utilities Expense	3,426.95				3,426.95			
37 Wage Expense	30,146.53		924.36		31,070.89			
38 Depreciation Expense			12,481.00		12,481.00			
39 Office Supplies Expense			909.56		909.56			
40 Store Sell Supp Expense			474.18		474.18			
41 Ship Sup & Postage Ex			137.99		137.99			
42 Insurance Expense			2,485.50		2,485.50			
43 Interest Expense			228.16		228.16			
44 Miscellaneous Expense	27.63				27.63			
	259,455.08	259,455.08	46,146.82	46,146.82	119,477.19	159,316.65	154,290.61	114,451.15
					39,839.46			39,839.46
					159,316.65	159,316.65	154,290.61	154,290.61

Adjustments: Allow for Bad Debts 2% of AR **Inventory** :$12,128.31 ,Office Supplies on Hand 953.92, Store Sell Supp on Hand 784.47, Shipping Supp on Hand 98.31, Postage on Hand 56.93 **Depreciation:** Truck 7,100.00 ,Office Equip 5,381.00 **Expired Insurance :** Office Ins $1,564.00 Truck Insurance 921.50 **Accrued Liabilities:** Interest Ex 228.16, Wage Ex 924.36

16.4			Hart & Sons				

GENERAL JOURNAL

Page_5

	DATE		DESCRIPTION	PR	DEBIT		CREDIT
1	*1999*		**Adusting Entries**				
2	Dec	31	Bad Debts Expense	535	740.53		
3			Allowance for Bad Debts	125			740.53
4			Office Supplies Expense	560	381.82		
5			Office Supplies Expense	130			381.82
6			Depreciation Expense	555	2,343.00		
7			Allow. Dep. Office EQ.	140			1,343.00
8			Allow. Dep. Delivery EQ.	155			1,000.00
9			Interest Expense	565	187.45		
10			Interest Payable	225			187.45
11			Wage Expense	545	1,496.50		
12			Wages Payable	230			1,496.50
13			Income Summary	330	8,000.00		
14			Inventory (old)	160			8,000.00
18			Inventory (new)	160	8,600.00		
19			Income Summary	330			8,600.00
20					*21,749.30*		*21,749.30*
21			**Closing Entries**				
22	Dec.	31	Sales	410	38,209.59		
23			Purchases Discount	515	347.44		
24			Purchases Returns and Allow.	520	693.00		
25			Income Summary	330			39,250.03
26			Income Summary	330	34,904.30		
27			Sales Discount	415			480.99
28			Sales Returns & Allowances	420			939.00
29			Purchases	510			23,736.60
30			Rent Expense	525			2,400.00
31			Employer Payroll Expense	530			301.60
32			Bad Debts Expense	535			740.53
33			Utilities Expense	540			520.00
34			Wages Expense	545			2,839.50
35			Depreciation Expense	555			2,343.00
36			Office Supplies Expense	560			410.80
37			Interest Expense	565			187.45
38			Miscellaneous Expense	575			4.83
			Income Summary	330	4,945.73		
			Capital	210			4,945.73
			Hart & Son, Capital	310	500.00		
			Hart & Son, Drawing	315			500.00
			Reversing Entries				
	Dec.	31	Interst Payable	225	187.45		
			Interest Expense	565			187.45
			Wages Payable	230	1,496.50		
			Wages Expense	545			1,496.50

12.4, 13.4, 14.4 15.4 & 16.4

HART & SON

Account   **CASH**   No. 110

DATE		ITEM	PR	Debit	Credit	BALANCE Debit	BALANCE Credit
Nov	1	BALANCE		26,568.14		26,568.14	
	30		1	13,168.22	29,072.60	10,663.76	
Dec	30		2	14,823.70	3,648.06	21,839.40	

Account   **CASH - PAYROLL**   No.115

DATE		ITEM	PR	Debit	Credit	BALANCE Debit	BALANCE Credit
Nov	27		1	1,117.49		1,117.49	
					1,117.49	0.00	

Account   **ACCOUNTS RECEIVABLE**   No. 120

DATE		ITEM	PR	Debit	Credit	BALANCE Debit	BALANCE Credit
Nov	14		1		12,389.00		12,389.00
	30		SJ 5	21,834.00		9,445.00	
Dec	1		1		442.00		
	1		1		9,003.00		
	13		2		283.00		
	13		2		5,314.91		
	21		2		214.00		
	30		SJ 5	14,609.59	15,256.91	8,797.68	

ALLOWANCE FOR DOUBTFUL ACCOUNTS   No.125

DATE		ITEM	PR	Debit	Credit	BALANCE Debit	BALANCE Credit
Nov	1	BALANCE			139.24		139.24
Dec	31	Adjusting Entry	5		740.53		879.77

16.4 Hart & Sons General Ledger page 2

Account OFFICE SUPPLIES — No. 130

DATE		ITEM	PR	Debit	Credit	BALANCE Debit	BALANCE Credit
Nov	1	BALANCE				321.82	
Dec	5		2	389.00		710.82	
	31	Adjusting Entry	5		381.82	329.00	

OFFICE EQUIPMENT — No.135

DATE		ITEM	PR	Debit	Credit	BALANCE Debit	BALANCE Credit
Nov	1	BALANCE				10,863.21	
	20		1	2,678.00		13,541.21	

ALLOWANCE FOR DEPRECIATION OFFICE EQUIPMENT — No. 140

DATE		ITEM	PR	Debit	Credit	BALANCE Debit	BALANCE Credit
Jan	1	BALANCE			2,683.21		2,683.21
Dec	31	Adjusting Entry	5		1,343.00		4,026.21

DELIVERY TRUCK — No. 150

DATE		ITEM	PR	Debit	Credit	BALANCE Debit	BALANCE Credit
Nov	13		1	27,000.00		27,000.00	

ALLOWANCE FOR DEPRECIATION DELIVERY TRUCK — No. 155

DATE		ITEM	PR	Debit	Credit	BALANCE Debit	BALANCE Credit
Dec	31	Adjusting Entry	5		1,000.00		1,000.00

Account INVENTORY — No. 160

DATE		ITEM	PR	Debit	Credit	BALANCE Debit	BALANCE Credit
Nov	1	BALANCE				8,000.00	
Dec	31	Adjusting Entry (old)	5		8,000.00		
	31	Adjusting Entry (new)	5	8,600.00		8,600.00	

Account **FEDERAL INCOME TAX PAYABLE** No. 205

DATE		ITEM	PR	Debit	Credit	BALANCE Debit	BALANCE Credit
Nov	27		1		98.50		98.50

Account **FICA PAYABLE** No. 207

DATE		ITEM	PR	Debit	Credit	BALANCE Debit	BALANCE Credit
Nov	27		1		114.83		114.83
			1		114.83		229.66

Account **MEDICARE PAYABLE** No. 208

DATE		ITEM	PR	Debit	Credit	BALANCE Debit	BALANCE Credit
Nov	27		1		12.18		12.18
	27		1		12.18		24.36

Account **ACCOUNTS PAYABLE** No. 210

DATE		ITEM	PR	Debit	Credit	BALANCE Debit	BALANCE Credit
Nov	1	BALANCE					1,000.00
	12		1	7,862.00		6,862.00	
	20		1		2,678.00	4,184.00	
	21		1	4,698.00			
	24		1	6,250.00			
Nov	30		PJ 3	10,948.00	18,810.00		3,678.00
Dec	5		2		389.00		4,067.00
	9		2	250.00			
	12		2	1,686.80			
	19		2	443.00			
	23		2	500.00			
	30		PJ 3	2,879.80	4,926.60		6,113.80

Account **FUTA PAYABLE** No. 220

DATE		ITEM	PR	Debit	Credit	BALANCE Debit	BALANCE Credit
Nov	27		1		107.44		107.44

Account — **STATE EMPLOYMENT PAYABLE** — No. 222

DATE		ITEM	PR	Debit	Credit	BALANCE Debit	BALANCE Credit
Nov	27		1		67.15		67.15

Account — **INTEREST PAYABLE** — No. 225

DATE		ITEM	PR	Debit	Credit	BALANCE Debit	BALANCE Credit
Dec	31	Adjusting Entry	5		187.45		187.45
	31	**Reversing Entry**	6	187.45		0.00	0.00

Account — **WAGES PAYABLE** — No. 230

DATE		ITEM	PR	Debit	Credit	BALANCE Debit	BALANCE Credit
Dec	31	Adjusting Entry	5		1,496.50		1,496.50
	31	**Reversing Entry**	6	1,496.50		0.00	0.00

Account — **NOTES PAYABLE** — No. 240

DATE		ITEM	PR	Debit	Credit	BALANCE Debit	BALANCE Credit
Nov	13		1		22,000.00		22,000.00
Nov	18		1	2,500.00			19,500.00

Account — **HART & SONS, CAPITAL** — No. 310

DATE		ITEM	PR	Debit	Credit	BALANCE Debit	BALANCE Credit
Nov	*1*	*BALANCE*					41,930.72
Dec	31	*Closing*	6		4,945.73		46,876.45
	31	*Closing*	6	500.00			46,376.45

Account — **HART & SONS, DRAWING** — No.315

DATE		ITEM	PR	Debit	Credit	BALANCE Debit	BALANCE Credit
Nov	26		1	500.00		500.00	
Dec	31	*Closing*	6		500.00	0.00	0.00

16.4 Hart & Sons General Ledger page 5

Account   **INCOME SUMMARY**   No. 330

DATE		ITEM	PR	Debit	Credit	BALANCE Debit	BALANCE Credit
Dec	31	Adjusting Entry	5	8,000.00		8,000.00	
	31	Adjusting Entry	5		8,600.00		600.00
Dec	31	*Closing*	6		39,250.03		39,850.03
	31	*Closing*	6	34,904.30			4,945.73
	31	*Closing*	6	4,945.75		0.00	0.00

Account   **SALES**   No. 410

DATE		ITEM	PR	Debit	Credit	BALANCE Debit	BALANCE Credit
Nov	7		1		555.00		555.00
	17		1		472.00		1,027.00
	30		SJ 5		21,834.00		22,861.00
Dec	6		2		739.00		23,600.00
	30		SJ 5		14,609.59		38,209.59
Dec	31	*Closing*	5	38,209.59		0.00	0.00

Account   **SALES DISCOUNT**   No. 415

DATE		ITEM	PR	Debit	Credit	BALANCE Debit	BALANCE Credit
Nov	14		1	247.78		247.78	
Dec	1		2	180.06		427.84	
	13		2	53.15		480.99	
Dec	31	*Closing*	5		480.99	0	0.00

Account   **SALES RETURNS & ALLOWANCES**   No. 420

DATE		ITEM	PR	Debit	Credit	BALANCE Debit	BALANCE Credit
Dec	1		2	442.00		442.00	
	13		2	283.00		725.00	
	21		2	214.00		939.00	
Dec	31	*Closing*	5		939.00	0.00	0.00

Account   **PURCHASES**   No. 510

DATE		ITEM	PR	Debit	Credit	BALANCE Debit	BALANCE Credit
Nov	30		PJ 3	18,810.00		18,810.00	
Dec	30		PJ 3	4,926.60		23,736.60	
Dec	31	*Closing*	5		23,736.60	0.00	0.00

| Account | | | | | PURCHASES DISCOUNT | | | No. 515 |

						BALANCE	
DATE		ITEM	PR	Debit	Credit	Debit	Credit
Nov	12		1		157.24		157.24
	21		1		93.96		251.20
	24		1		62.50		313.70
	12		2		33.74		347.44
Dec	31	*Closing*	5	347.44		0.00	0.00

| Account | | | | | PURCHASES RETURNS & ALLOWANCES | | | No. 520 |

						BALANCE	
DATE		ITEM	PR	Debit	Credit	Debit	Credit
Dec	9		2		250.00		250.00
	19		2		443.00		693.00
Dec	31	*Closing*	5	693.00		0.00	0.00

| Account | | | | | RENT EXPENSE | | | No. 525 |

						BALANCE	
DATE		ITEM	PR	Debit	Credit	Debit	Credit
Nov	3		1	1,200.00		1,200.00	
Dec	3		2	1,200.00		2,400.00	
Dec	31	*Closing*	5		2,400.00	0.00	0.00

| Account | | | | | EMPLOYER PAYROLL EXPENSE | | | No. 530 |

						BALANCE	
DATE		ITEM	PR	Debit	Credit	Debit	Credit
Nov	27		1	301.60		301.60	
Dec	31	*Closing*	5		301.60	0.00	0.00

| Account | | | | | DOUBTFUL ACCOUNTS EXPENSE | | | No. 535 |

						BALANCE	
DATE		ITEM	PR	Debit	Credit	Debit	Credit
Dec	31	Adjusting Entry	5	740.53		740.53	
Dec	31	*Closing*	5		740.53	0.00	0.00

| Account | | | | | UTILITIES EXPENSE | | | No. 540 |

						BALANCE	
DATE		ITEM	PR	Debit	Credit	Debit	Credit
Nov	16		1	225.00		225.00	
	20		2	295.00		520.00	
Dec	31	*Closing*	5		520	0	0.00

Account				WAGE EXPENSE				No. 545	
								BALANCE	
DATE		**ITEM**	**PR**	**Debit**	**Credit**			**Debit**	**Credit**
Nov	27		1	1,343.00				1,343.00	
Dec	31	Adjusting	5	1,496.50				2,839.50	
	31	*Closing*	5		2,839.50			0.00	0.00
Jan	1	**Reversing**	6		1,496.50				1,496.50

Account				DEPRECIAITON EXPENSE				No. 555	
								BALANCE	
DATE		**ITEM**	**PR**	**Debit**	**Credit**			**Debit**	**Credit**
Dec	31	Adjusting	5	2,343.00				2,343.00	
	31	*Closing*	5		2,343.00			0.00	0.00

Account				OFFICE SUPPLIES EXPENSE				No. 560	
								BALANCE	
DATE		**ITEM**	**PR**	**Debit**	**Credit**			**Debit**	**Credit**
Nov	25		1	28.98				28.98	
Dec	31	Adjusting	5	381.82				410.80	
	31	*Closing*	5		410.80			0.00	0.00

Account				INTEREST EXPENSE				No. 565	
								BALANCE	
DATE		**ITEM**	**PR**	**Debit**	**Credit**			**Debit**	**Credit**
Dec	31	Adjusting	5	187.45					
	31	*Closing*	5		187.45			0.00	0.00
Jan	1	**Reversing**	6		187.45				187.45

Account				MISCELLANEOUS EXPENSE				No. 575	
								BALANCE	
DATE		**ITEM**	**PR**	**Debit**	**Credit**			**Debit**	**Credit**
Nov	25		1	4.83				4.83	
Dec	31	*Closing*	6		4.83			0.00	0.00

HART & SON

16.4   **Post Closing Trial Balance**

December 31,------

	ACCOUNT NAME	DEBIT	CREDIT
1	Cash	21,839.40	
2	Accounts Receivable	8,797.68	
3	Allowance for Doubtful Accounts		879.77
4	Office Supplies	329.00	
5	Office Equipment	13,541.21	
6	Allowance for Depreciation of Office EQ		4,026.21
7	Delivery Truck	27,000.00	
8	Allowance for Depreciation of Delivery Truck		1,000.00
9	Inventory	8,600.00	
10	Federal Income Tax Payable		98.50
11	FICA Payable		229.66
12	Medicare Payable		24.36
13	Accounts Payable		6,113.80
14	FUTA Payable		107.44
15	State Employment Payable		67.15
16	Interst Payable		187.45
17	Wages Payable		1,496.50
18	Notes Payable		19,500.00
19	Hart & Sons, Capital		46,376.45
20		$80,107.29	$80,107.29
21			
22			
23			
24			
25			

Meg's Muffler Shop

17.1

CALCULATIONS					GENERAL JOURNAL			

Wk	Gross Receipts	Rate	Sales	Tax		Accounts	Debit	Credit
1	$1,628.18	8.5	$1,500.63	$127.55				
					1	Cash	1,628.18	
2	$1,987.95	8.5	$1,832.21	$155.74		Sales		1,500.63
						Sales Tax Payable		127.55
3	$2,382.38	8.5	$2,195.74	$186.64	2	Cash	1,987.95	
						Sales		1,832.21
4	$1,831.96	8.5	$1,688.44	$143.52		Sales Tax Payable		155.74
					3	Cash	2,382.38	
Sales		100%				Sales		2,195.74
Tax		8.50%			4	Sales Tax Payable		186.64
Sales and Tax		1.085				Cash	1,831.96	
						Sales		1,688.44
						Sales Tax Payable		143.52

Meg's Muffler Shop
Total price of the job plus tax is rung up as
the sale. Therefore, Divide amount rung up

Marquita's Boutique

17.2

Date	Gross Receipts	Rate	Sales	Tax
7/25	798.43	8.50	735.88	62.55
7/26	2,289.35	8.50	2,110.00	179.35

Cash journal entries for Marquita's Boutique are on
Page 2 Solutions 17.2

| 17.2 | | | | Marquita's Boutique CASH JOURNAL | Page 1 | | |

	CASH		DATE		DESCRIPTION	Post	GENERAL	
	Debit	Credit	Month	Day		Ref	Debit	Credit
1	469.26		July	5	Sales			432.50
2					Sales Tax Payable			36.76
3				8	Credit Card Receivable		4,230.42	
4					Sales			3,899.00
5					Sales Tax Payable			331.42
6	4,145.81			9	Credit Card Fees		84.61	
7					Credit Card Receivable			4,230.42
8	417.67			12	Sales			384.95
9					Sales Tax Payable			32.72
10				15	Credit Card Receivable		2,781.94	
11					Sales			2,564.00
12					Sales Tax Payable			217.94
13	2,726.30			16	Credit Card Fees		55.64	
14					Credit Card Receivable			2,781.94
15	798.43			25	Sales			735.88
16					Sales Tax Payable			62.55
17				26	Credit Card Receivable		2,289.35	
18					Sales			2,110.00
19					Sales Tax Payable			179.35
20	2,243.56			27	Credit Card Fees		45.79	
21					Credit Card Receivable			2,289.35
22								
23								
24	10,801.03						9,487.75	20,288.78
25								

MOLLY ELOISE MATERIALS
Income Statement
For the Month of December

#17.3

	DESCRIPTION			
1	Sales		153,735.06	
2	Less Sales Discount		2,538.16	
3	Sales Returns and Allowances		4,147.75	
4	Gross Sales			147,049.15
5	Cost of Good Sold			
6	Beginning Inventory		15,698.56	
7	Plus Purchases		46,315.43	
8	Less Purchases Discount		2,189.51	
9	Purchases Returns and Allowances		3,392.08	
10	Merchandise Available for Sale		56,432.40	
11	Less Ending Inventory		12,128.31	
12	Cost of Good Sold			44,304.09
13	Gross Income from Sales			102,745.06
14	Operating Expenses			
15	Rent Expense		8,600.00	
16	Employer Payroll Expense		3,308.90	
17	Bat Debts Expense		679.20	
18	Utilities Expense		3,426.95	
19	Wage Expense		30,146.53	
20	Depreciation Exepense		12,481.00	
21	Office Supplies Expense		909.56	
22	Store Selling Supplies Expense		474.18	
23	Shipping Supplies and Postage		137.99	
24	Insurance Expense		2485.5	
25	Miscellaneous Expense		27.63	
26	Total Operating Expenses			62,677.44
27	Gross Income			40,067.62
28	**Other Expenses**			
29	Interest Expense			228.16
30	Net Income			$39,839.46

MOLLY ELOISE MATERIALS

Capital Statement

December 31, ------

Beginning Capital			31,069.39
Net Income		39,839.46	
Less Drawing		-3,385.00	
Change in Capital			36,454.46
Capial October 31, 1999			$67,523.85

MOLLY ELOISE MATERIALS

Balance Sheet

December 31,-------

Assets			
Cash		33,673.21	
Accounts Receivable	35,385.13		
Allowance of Doubtful Accouns	707.70	34,677.43	
Office Supplies		953.92	
Store Selling Supplies		784.47	
Shipping Supplies		98.30	
Postage		56.93	
Pre-Paid Insurance Office		857.55	
Pre-Paid Insurance Truck		921.50	
Office Equipment	25,681.29		
Allowance for Depreciation	15,719.25	9,962.04	
Delivery Truck	40,365.00		
Allowance for Depreciation	21,300.00	19,065.00	
Inventory		12,128.31	
Total Assets			$113,178.66
Liabilities			
Federal income Tax Payale		3,851.87	
FICA Payable		1,764.10	
Medicare Payable		185.43	
Accounts Payable		8,879.62	
FUTA Payable		2,461.76	
State Employment Payable		1,527.91	
Interest Payable		228.16	
Wages Payable		924.36	
Notes Payable		25,831.60	
Total Liabilities			45,654.81
Capital			
Molly Eloise, Capital			67,523.85
Total Capital and Liabilities			$113,178.66

18.1   Mallett and Foote
GENERAL JOURNAL

Page_5

	DATE		DESCRIPTION	PR	DEBIT	CREDIT
1			**Beginning investment**			
2	July	`1	Cash		2,000.00	
3			Mowing Equipment		8,000.00	
4			Capital, Liam Foote			10,000.00
5		1	Cash		5,610.00	
6			Mowing Equipment		1,000.00	
7			Yard Equipment		1,990.00	
8			Trailer		1,400.00	
9			Capital, Raleigh Mallett			10,000.00
10						
11						
12						

CAPITAL STATEMENT
MALLETT AND FOOTE PARTNERSHIP

DECEMBER

			Statement for Liam Foote			
	Beginning Capital					10,000.00
		Net Income			5,200.00	
		Less Drawing			1,250.00	
	Change in Capital					3,950.00
	Ending Capital					$13,950.00
			Statement for Raleigh Mallett			
	Beginning Capital					10,000.00
		Net Income			5,200.00	
		Less Drawing			2,400.00	
	Change in Capital					2,800.00
	Ending Capital					$12,800.00

We Care Lawn Care
GENERAL JOURNAL

18.2

Page_5

	DATE		DESCRIPTION	PR	DEBIT	CREDIT
1	May	1	Subscriptions Receivable		65,000.00	
2			Capital Stock Subscribed			65,000.00
3			**Note**: I. Foote 25,000, R. Mallett 25,000			
4			M. Foote 5,000 K. Foote 10,000			
5						
6		3	Cash		20,000.00	
7			Capital Stock			20,000.00
8						
9		5	Cash		40,000.00	
10			Subscriptions Receivable			40,000.00
11			**Note**: I. Foote 15,000, R. Mallett 10,000			
12			M. Foote 5,000 K. Foote 10,000			
13			Capital Stock Subscribed		40,000.00	
14			Capital Stock			40,000.00
18						
19		15	Cash		25,000.00	
20			Capital Stock Subscribed		25,000.00	
21			Subscriptions Receivable			25,000.00
22			Capital Stock			25,000.00
23			**Note**: I. Foote 10,000, R. Mallett 15,000			
24						
25						

18.3 MOLLY ELOISE MATERIALS
GENERAL JOURNAL

Page_20

	DATE		DESCRIPTION	PR	DEBIT	CREDIT
1	2000		**Adusting Entries**			
2	Dec	31	Bad Debts Expense		679.20	
3			Allowance for Bad Debts			679.20
4			Office Supplies Expense		909.56	
5			Office Supplies			909.56
6			Store Selling Supplies Expense		474.18	
7			Store Selling Supplies			474.18
8			Shipping and Postage Expense		137.99	
9			Shipping Supplies			84.92
10			Postage			53.07
11			Insurance Expense		2,485.50	
12			Pre-Paid Insurance Office			1,564.00
13			Pre-Paid Insurance Truck			921.50
14			Depreciation Expense		12,481.00	
15			Allow. Dep. Office EQ.			5,381.00
16			Allow. Dep. Delivery EQ.			7,100.00
17			Interest Expense		228.16	
18			Interest Payable			228.16
19			Wage Expense		924.36	
20			Wages Payable			924.36
21			Income Summary		15,698.56	
22			Inventory (old)			15,698.56
23			Inventory (new)		12,128.31	
24			Income Summary			12,128.31
					46,146.82	46,146.82

	18.3		MOLLY ELOISE MATERIALS				
			GENERAL JOURNAL				
						Page_21	
	DATE		DESCRIPTION	PR	DEBIT		CREDIT
1			**Closing Entries**				
2	Dec.	31	Sales		153,735.06		
3			Purchases Discount		2,189.51		
4			Purchases Returns and Allow.		3,392.08		
5			Income Summary				159,316.65
6			Income Summary		115,906.94		
7			Sales Discount				2,538.16
8			Sales Returns & Allowances				4,147.75
9			Purchases				46,315.43
10			Rent Expense				8,600.00
11			Employer Payroll Expense				2,384.54
12			Bad Debts Expense				679.20
13			Utilities Expense				3,426.95
14			Wages Expense				31,070.89
15			Depreciation Expense				12,481.00
16			Office Supplies Expense				909.56
17			Store Sell Sup Expense				474.18
18			Ship Sup & Postage Expense				137.99
19			Insurance Expenese				2,485.50
20			Interest Expense				228.16
21			Miscellaneous Expense				27.63
22					$275,223.59		$275,223.59
23							
24			Income Summary		39,839.46		
25			Capital				39,839.46
26			Hart & Son, Capital		3,385.00		
27			Hart & Son, Drawing				3,385.00
28							
29			**Reversing Entries**				
30	Dec.	31	Interst Payable		228.16		
31			Interest Expense				228.16
33			Wages Payable		924.36		
29			Wages Expense				924.36
30							
32					$44,376.98		$44,376.98
33